EDINBURGH UNIVERSITY PUBLICATIONS

History, Philosophy and Economics

NO. 7

Europe as queen, from S. Münster, *Cosmographia*, 1588. See p. 119.

EUROPE

THE EMERGENCE OF AN IDEA

DENYS HAY M.A.

Professor of Mediaeval History, University of Edinburgh

EDINBURGH
AT THE UNIVERSITY PRESS
1957

THE EDINBURGH UNIVERSITY PRESS

Agents

THOMAS NELSON AND SONS LTD
Parkside Works Edinburgh 9
36 Park Street London W1
312 Flinders Street Melbourne C1

302-304 Barclays Bank Building
Commissioner and Kruis Streets
Johannesburg

THOMAS NELSON AND SONS (CANADA) LTD
91-93 Wellington Street West Toronto 1

THOMAS NELSON AND SONS
19 East 47th Street New York 17

SOCIÉTÉ FRANÇAIS D'EDITIONS NELSON
25 rue Henri Barbusse Paris V^e

PRINTED IN GREAT BRITAIN BY
ROBERT CUNNINGHAM AND SONS LTD.
ALVA, SCOTLAND

CONTENTS

		page
	Preface	ix
chap.		
1.	Europa and Japheth	1
2.	Christendom	16
3.	The medieval notion of Europe and its peoples	37
4.	The disintegration of Christendom	56
5.	The emergence of Europe	73
6.	Renaissance Christendom	96
7.	The prospect of Europe	117
	Index	126

PLATES

'Europe', from the 1588 reprint of Münster's
Cosmographia   *Frontispiece*

I. (*a*) The Rape of Europa   *facing page* 4

(*b*) A T-and-O map   4

II. A portion of a fifteenth-century Portolan   20

III. Noah drunk, from the Schedel Chronicle   84

IV. Galle's Europe from the *Prosopographia*   100

V. Hondius's map of world religions   *bet. pp.* 108-9

LIST OF ABBREVIATIONS

C.F.M.A.   Les classiques français du moyen âge

C.H.F.M.A. Les classiques de l'histoire de France au
            moyen âge

E.E.T.S.   Early English Text Society

M.G.H.   Monumenta Germaniae Historica

P.L.   J. P. Migne, *Patrologia Latina*

R.S.   Rolls Series

S.A.T.F.   Société des anciens textes français

PREFACE

IT is, I suppose, a common experience for historians to embark on the study of a subject feeling that no one else is interested in it, only to discover much later that other scholars are at work on the same or parallel problems. This has certainly happened in the case of this essay. I began collecting material in 1948 and for a considerable time came on no other historical studies germane to my enquiry. It was only when I began putting my notes together in the summer of 1954 that I discovered the valuable studies of Fritzemeyer, Chabod, Saitta and Gollwitzer, which are referred to below (p. 117). Fortunately these works are all primarily concerned with developments in the seventeenth and later centuries, a period not covered by my own research, and which I only touch on briefly in my concluding chapter.

This short book is emphatically restricted to the *emergence* of the idea of Europe, not to its full development in and after the eighteenth century. It is also not concerned with the larger questions of the validity of European history. Whether or not Europe is 'an intelligible field of study' has been discussed by Professor A. J. Toynbee in his *Study of History* (1934-54), by Professor O. Halecki, *The Limits and Divisions of European History* (1950), by Professor G. Barraclough, *History in a Changing World* (1955), by their numerous critics and by others. Such matters are not without their bearing on the theme of this book, but my aim is quite different and much more modest.

I began because I was struck by the relative frequency of the word Europe in the texts of the later middle ages.

I detected in that period a gradual consciousness of Europe as more than a mere geographical term. Further investigation of this, and of the rapidly extending employment of the word in the Renaissance centuries, led me to conclude that in this development it was the virtual identification of Europe with an earlier Christendom which was the most influential single factor. I accordingly tried to investigate the emergence of the notion of Christendom. Behind that in turn lay the cosmography of the ancient world and that, too, had briefly to be considered, for it was the Greeks who first used Europe in a geographical and political sense.

Much of what follows, therefore, might be described, in Marc Bloch's phrase, as 'historical semantics'—an attempt to catch the words of the past and the sense in which they were used from time to time. Such an investigation could clearly be endless: there are always more texts to be read and further illustrations to be gleaned which might amplify or modify conclusions already reached. In deciding to publish now I do so in the full realization that much more remains to be found out about the concepts whose history is here attempted and in the hope that others may be prompted to question my argument and furnish other references. The way in which the idea of Europe grew is clearly of great interest because of its importance in modern history and contemporary politics.

I have bothered a good many experts in the course of working on this subject and I have tried to acknowledge such help at appropriate points in what follows. But I must extend more general thanks to the staff of Edinburgh University Library, to Mr. G. R. Crone of the Royal Geographical Society, to Mr. J. C. Maxwell and the learned reader of the University Press. To the staff of the Warburg Institute, London University, I have been especially troublesome, and I am very conscious of what I owe to them. I have to thank Lt.-Col. G. W. Meates,

F.S.A., for permission to reproduce the Lullingstone 'Rape of Europa'.

The substance of Chapter 5 was delivered as a lecture to the Tenth International Congress of Historical Sciences, Rome, September 1955, and is summarized in an article in *Diogène* (Paris), no. 17, January 1957, pp. 50-62.

DENYS HAY

Edinburgh
April, 1957

E.S.A., the permission to reproduce the following map of Europe.

The substance of Chapter 1 was delivered as a lecture to the French Geographical Society at Grenoble and printed in Revue September 1955, and is transcribed here in article in Congress Paris, no. 2, January 1977, pp. 30-63.

Edinburgh
April, 1977

CHAPTER I

EUROPA AND JAPHETH

FOR the Greeks, as later for the Romans, the word Europe was associated in the first place with myth rather than science.

Europa was the daughter of Agenor king of Tyre, situated on the coast of what we now call the Lebanon, the Phoenicia of the ancients. Zeus fell in love with her. To possess her he turned himself into a splendid bull and presented himself on the shore where Europa and her maidens were playing. The maiden was attracted by the beast and mounted on its back. The bull then plunged into the sea, carrying its beautiful load westwards to Crete. There Europa became by Zeus the mother of several sons and later married the king of Crete. This story is only part of a group of related legends—the search for Europa made by her brothers, the adventures of her sons Minos, Rhadamanthus and Sarpedon—which do not concern us, but which form a not inconsiderable part of the corpus of classical mythology.

Does the migration of Europa throw light on the geographical use of the word Europe? An earlier generation of scholars might have been prepared to see in it a dramatized account of the transference of a Semitic word for the land of the setting sun or of darkness (*erib*) westwards into Greek usage. Recently this view has been largely abandoned and Europe has been derived from Greek roots. These suggest the meaning 'broadfaced'. If the Semitic root for the word is not correct, etymology has little to tell us of the adoption of the word for the description of a part of the surface of the earth.[1]

[1] On these matters see Pauly-Wissowa, *Real-Encyclopaedie für classischen*

The matter puzzled the Greeks.[1]

In surviving sources this territorial meaning applied the term Europe to the mainland of Greece, in opposition to the Aegean islands. This is the sense the word has in the post-Homeric *Hymn to Apollo*. It was soon extended to the whole of continental Greece and then to areas west and north as the Greek colonization of the Mediterranean proceeded. During the ninth to sixth centuries B.C., when this colonization was most active, the terms Asia and Libya also gained currency. At first Greek speculation accepted only two great divisions, a western and an eastern, Europe and Asia (Libya being a subdivision of the latter). This seems to have been the position of Hecataeus of Miletus, who flourished about 500 B.C., but in the next generation Herodotus scouted this view and accepted without question a tripartite division of the *oecumene*, the habitable globe.[2] The boundaries were at first not absolutely clear: it was debated whether the Nile was the boundary between Asia and Africa or the isthmus of Suez; and for a while the small river Phasis, which flowed into the eastern end of the Black Sea, was regarded as the true boundary between Europe and Asia, before this became established as falling at the Tanais river (Don).

In a sense two continents suited the Greeks better than three. This is particularly evident in Herodotus himself. In so far as the Greeks had a sense of fundamental contin-

Altertumswissenschaft, vi (1) 1287, 1298-9, and J. Oliver Thomson, *History of Ancient Geography*, Cambridge 1948, pp. 21, 396 and literature there quoted; H. J. Rose, *A Handbook of Greek Mythology*, London 1928, pp. 182-3: Europa is 'probably no more than the eponym of the continent of Europe'. The most recent discussion is by Franz Miltner, 'Aus der Frühgeschichte des Namens Europa, *Orpheus*, i (1954), 14-21. A distinct myth made Europa daughter of Oceanus and Tethys, with Asia and Libya as her half-sisters.

[1] 'For my part I cannot conceive why three names [Europa, Asia, Libya], and women's names especially, should ever have been given to a tract which is in reality one', Herodotus (trans. Rawlinson), iv. 45.

[2] J. Oliver Thomson's book, cited above, supersedes all other accounts of ancient geography in English, except E. H. Bunbury, *History of Ancient Geography*, 2 vols., London 1879, with its very full documentation; for late antiquity see vol. i of C. R. Beazley's book, cited below, p. 37. The texts are collected and translated in E. H. Warmington, *Greek Geography*, London 1934.

ental differences these lay between East and West, between Persian and Greek, between Asia and Europe. Herodotus explained his purpose in writing in such terms. It was to preserve

from decay the remembrance of what men have done, and of preventing the great and wonderful actions of the Greeks and the Barbarians from losing their due meed of glory; and withal to put on record what were their grounds of feud.[1]

By the fifth century 'Asiatic' was firmly linked with concepts of lavish splendour, of vulgarity, of arbitrary authority, of all that was antithetical to Greece and Greek values. Yet despite this opposition it seems that Europe and Asia as individual regions did not hold much active *political* meaning for a Greek. They did for a time in the writings of Isocrates (d. 338 B.C.), due to the virtual identification of Europe with Greece, of Asia with Persia.[2]

To these antitheses, however, formal geographical speculation did not give much support in Greek antiquity, though so little was known by Greeks of the world at large that they might have been excused for elaborating an ideal description which would have exalted Europe above the other continents. Some tentative steps in this direction were taken. The writer of the study *Influences of Atmosphere, Water and Situation*, which is attributed to the school of Hippocrates (fifth century B.C.) praises the climate and natural geography of Greece and contrasts the climate of Asia in favour of the former; similar notions are found in Herodotus and Aristotle; and by the time of Strabo Europe and its peoples are regarded as the best favoured by circumstances.[3]

[1] Proem to book i. A. J. Toynbee deals trenchantly with Herodotus's part in diffusing the notion of an antithesis between Europe and Asia, *A Study in History*, viii. 708-11.

[2] Arnaldo Momigliano, 'L'Europa come concetto politico presso Isocrate e gli Isocratei', *Rivista di filologia e d'istruzione classica*, lxi (1933), pp. 477-87, esp. pp. 480-2. Professor Momigliano and Mr. W. K. Smith have both been good enough to read and comment on this chapter.

[3] Thomson, 106-8, 254-5, 322; see the extracts translated by A. J. Toynbee, *Greek Historical Thought*, London 1924, pp. 165-8, and Warmington, pp. 54-9. The quotation from Aristotle is below, p. 5.

The notion of the tripartite *oecumene* of the Greeks was accepted by Roman writers. The extension of Roman control over Spain, Gaul and Britain led to an enormous increase in knowledge about the continent of Europe, though the Romans scarcely did more than maintain the knowledge of the East which had been acquired by the Greeks of the Hellenistic period, and the third continent— whose name the Romans changed from Libya to Africa —continued to be known only on its Mediterranean edge, apart from the valley of the Nile and the Red Sea coast. Equally the Romans accepted the East-West polarity of the Greeks, though it had less relevance for them[1] and 'Asiatic' tended to become pejorative only in a literary sense—bombastic and over elaborate composition could be thus described.

Yet for neither Greeks nor Romans did Europe mean much. Fear of Persia lent colour to the Greek attitude to the continents, but the empire of Alexander the Great was in Asia, not Europe, while the remnants of this were conquered by a Rome which made its greatest advances in the north and west of Europe. What cemented together the Greek World and after it the world of Rome was the inland sea, which linked all but the remotest provinces, which was literally the cradle of Greek civilization and which even the Romans, averse as they were to maritime adventure, annexed as 'Mare nostrum'. Beyond the serenity of the Mediterranean (as later ages were to call it)[2] and the outposts of order carried outwards by the Mediterranean conquerors, Greek or Roman, lay barbarism. Barbarians, as the Romans knew well enough, were confined to no particular continents, and were particularly troublesome in Europe itself. For a Greek Greece itself

[1] The Romans regarded Carthage in somewhat the same light as the Greeks had regarded Persia; but the hatred was not extended to the whole continent and it was 'Carthaginian' which acquired a harmful connotation in Latin, not 'African'.

[2] *Mediterraneum mare* occurs for the first time in Solinus (see Bunbury, ii. 679n. and passage quoted below, p. 7); a sea-change indeed for an adjective which had earlier meant the opposite of maritime.

PLATE I(*a*). 'Rape of Europa'. Mosaic at Roman Villa, Lullingstone.
(Courtesy of Lt. Col. G. W. Meates). See p. 5, n. 2.

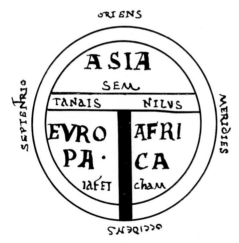

PLATE I(*b*). A T-O Map from an eleventh-century manuscript of Isidore.
(Andrews Collection, Royal Geographical Society). See p. 54.

was the heart of civilization; for a Roman Rome occupied the same place. Aristotle, indeed, so far from extending the continental convention, followed the lead of
Hippocrates and positively erected Greece into an entity
comparable to Europe and Asia. This is how he speaks of
the character of men in relation to their environment:

Those who live in a cold climate and in Europe are full of spirit,
but wanting in intelligence and skill; and therefore they keep their
freedom, but have no political organization, and are incapable of
ruling over others. Whereas the natives of Asia are intelligent and
inventive, but they are wanting in spirit, and therefore they are
always in a state of subjection and slavery. But the Hellenic race,
which is situated between them, is likewise intermediate in character,
being high-spirited and also intelligent.[1]

Similarly for a Roman, the boundary that mattered was
not the Don, but the strategic frontier of the Rhine and
the Danube. When artists in classical antiquity represented Europa it was the maiden they normally saw,
devoid of any continental overtones, a symbol of passion
rather than politics.[2] Pictures of the personified continent
are rare. Only one seems to possess any emotional content. This is a first-century B.C. marble relief[3] commem-
orating the battle of Arbela, where Alexander the Great
defeated the Persians in 331 B.C. The picture should thus
be linked with the brief period of interest in the political
character of Europe which we have at the time of Isocrates.

A minor reason for the relative lack of emotional content in the use of Europe, Asia and Africa during classical
times was the absence of large scale maps. Certainly

[1] *Politics* 1327b; trans. B. Jowett, vii. 7; cf. 1285a, iii. 14, § 6. In the passage
quoted Jowett glossed 'Europe' by prefacing '[northern]' to the word.
[2] See plate I (*a*), a British example of the rape of Europa, the mosaic in the
Roman villa at Lullingstone. The fullest study of this subject is by O. Jahn,
'Die Entführung der Europa auf antiken Kunstwerken', *Denkschriften der Kaiser-
lichen Akademie der Wissenschaften*, Phil.-Hist. Classe, Bd. xix, Vienna 1870,
pp. 1–54, with an appendix in which a large number of reproductions are given.
Cf. the discussion in R. Hinks, *Myth and Allegory in Ancient Art*, London 1939,
pp. 65–6 (where a lively portrayal of antithesis between Hellas and Asia is
analysed) and p. 73. Europa as a pictorial subject occurs in Ovid, *Metamor-
phoses*, vi. 104, the story in ii. 834–75.
[3] Now in the Palazzo Chigi, Rome. Illustrated in Hinks, plate 9.

B

compared with later ages there seems to have been singularly little incentive to the production of visual representations of the *oecumene* or *orbis*. We can reconstruct the
world-pictures of Herodotus or Strabo but we cannot
confidently assume that they habitually saw the world in
a two-dimensional way. As for the Romans, there is
evidence that a few maps were constructed, but if they
were like those that have survived in the Peutinger tables
they were little more than diagrammatic representations
of the roads of the Empire—which is after all what one
would have expected. Perhaps the mariners of ancient
times had charts. The *periploi*, or coastal itineraries, survive in literary form only but may have been originally
constructed in the form of maps. Local plans, of course,
were frequently made of towns or irrigation systems or
a network of communications. But the general depiction
of the world at large seems to have been restricted to the
works of a handful of scientific geographers and astron-
omers.

These maps, little as they seem to have influenced the
general attitude of ordinary folk in ancient times, are none
the less important, for they provided the essentials of later
cartography. The world was seen, when thus represented,
as circular. Round the inhabited continents ran a surround-
ing ocean, and the Mediterranean provided an axis for
the map maker, who visualized an arrangement of land
masses round it in roughly symmetrical fashion: Europe
and Africa to north and south of the inland sea and
approximately equalling together in mass Asia to the east.
Such simplifications were not without their critics, who
became even more sceptical as the sphericity of the earth
became an established fact with Aristotle. From Eratosthenes (*c.* 200 B.C.) onwards the technical problems of
depicting accurately a spherical surface in a two dimen-
sional form attracted scientific interest, culminating in the
great work of Ptolemy (second century A.D.). But
Ptolemy, though he abandoned the circumambient ocean,

the symmetrical land masses and other non-scientific assumptions, was neglected in his own day and later. The latter-day Romans read not Ptolemy but his contemporary Solinus and it was his confused, unscholarly and ill-informed views which best represent the picture of the world commonly held in late antiquity.

The Straits of Gibraltar admit the Atlantic ocean into our sea as a dividing line in the inhabited earth. For the Ocean coming in from the West sweeps against Europe on the left side and Africa on the right. It divides the mountains Calpe and Abinna, which are called the columns of Hercules, and spreads out between Spain and the land of the Moors. And at the Straits, like a door, opens the threshold of the interior sea, where the Ocean, mingling with the lesser seas of the Mediterranean, goes on to the East. . . . This is in the heart of the land mass. The Ocean, however, embraces the outermost shores, being named from the regions it touches, Arabic, Persian, Indian, Oriental, Chinese, Hyrcanian, Caspian, Scythian, German, Gallic, Atlantic, Libyan and Aegyptian.[1]

Into a world conceived in this fashion, the three continents being divided by the Mediterranean, the Don and the Nile, the whole being surrounded by the circumambient Ocean, came the Jewish cosmogony and the attitudes to nature engendered by the new religion of Christianity.

The Jew and the Christian of the eastern Mediterranean were exposed to all the traditions of the Graeco-Roman world, yet bound by a scheme of creation and a view of nature which were laid down in immutable scriptures. The Bible and the accepted view of the world we have been discussing were, in fact, hardly at odds. The Hebrew tradition viewed the earth as circular: Isaiah speaks of the 'circle of the earth' and in Proverbs creation is described

[1] A free and abbreviated rendering of Solinus (ed. Mommsen) 23. 13-18: Sed Gaditanum fretum, a Gadibus dictum, Atlanticos aestus in nostrum mare discidio inmittit orbis. nam Oceanus, quem Graii sic nominant de celeritate, ab occasu solis inrumpens laevo latere Europam radit, Africam dextero, scissisque Calpe et Abinna montibus quos dicunt columnas Herculis, inter Mauros funditur et Hispaniam: ac freto isti . . . quodam ostio aperit limen interni aequoris, mixtus mediterraneis sinibus quos ad usque orientem propellit. . . . haec in gremiis terrarum. oras autem extimas Oceanus amplectitur, qui a litoribus suis Arabicus Persicus Indicus Eous Sericus Hyrcanus Caspius Scythicus Germanicus Gallicus Atlanticus Libycus Aegyptius dicitur.

as setting 'a circle on the face of the deep'.[1] Nor was it difficult to accommodate the knowledge that Jerusalem was the centre of the world, for the eastern Mediterranean was already the area from which knowledge of the earth's surface radiated out.[2] There were certain features of Christian-Jewish topography that were awkward (the situation of the garden of Eden, the location of Gog and Magog) but they would have been troublesome in any geographical system.[3] Above all it proved feasible to adjust the three continents of pagan antiquity to the threefold division of the world among the sons of Noah.

As much was to depend on the speculation provoked by the ninth and tenth chapters of Genesis they shall be summarized here.

Genesis, chapter 9

18. And the sons of Noah, that went forth of the ark, were Shem, and Ham, and Japheth: and Ham is the father of Canaan.

19. These are the three sons of Noah: and of them was the whole earth overspread.

20. And Noah began to be an husbandman, and he planted a vineyard:

21. And he drank of the wine, and was drunken: and he was uncovered within his tent.

22. And Ham, the father of Canaan, saw the nakedness of his father, and told his two brethren without.

23. And Shem and Japheth took a garment, and laid it upon both their shoulders, and went backward, and covered the nakedness of their father; and their faces were backward, and they saw not their father's nakedness.

24. And Noah awoke from his wine, and knew what his younger son had done unto him.

25. And he said, Cursed be Canaan; a servant of servants shall he be unto his brethren.

26. And he said, Blessed be the Lord God of Shem; and Canaan shall be his servant.

27. God shall enlarge Japheth, and he shall dwell in the tents of Shem; and Canaan shall be his servant. . . .

[1] Isaiah xl. 22, Prov. viii. 27-9.

[2] Ezekiel v. 5: 'I have set it in the midst of the nations, and countries that are round about her'; xxxviii. 12 (umbilicus terrae).

[3] On such 'errors' see A. D. White, *A history of the warfare of Science with Theology in Christendom*, 2 vols., New York 1897, i. 98-102.

Chapter 10

1. Now these are the generations of the sons of Noah, Shem, Ham, and Japheth: and unto them were sons born after the flood.

2. The sons of Japheth; Gomer . . .

5. By these were the isles of the Gentiles divided in their lands; every one after his tongue, after their families, in their nations.

6. And the sons of Ham; Cush . . . and Canaan.

8. And Cush begat Nimrod. . . .

10. And the beginning of his kingdom was Babel, and Erech, and Accad, and Calneh, in the land of Shinar.

19. And the border of the Canaanites was from Sidon, as thou comest to Gerar, unto Gaza; as thou goest, unto Sodom, and Gomorrah, and Admah, and Zeboim, even unto Lasha.

21. Unto Shem also, the father of all the children of Eber, the brother of Japheth the elder, even to him were children born.

22. The children of Shem; Elam . . .

30. And their dwelling was from Mesha, as thou goest unto Sephar a mount of the east.[1]

The first adaptation of this material to the Hellenistic view of the world was made by Josephus, a scholarly Jew whose active life covers the middle and later decades of the first century A.D. Though by no means a supporter of Jewish irredentism, Josephus was anxious to defend the cultural autonomy of his people, to establish the independent value of Jewish tradition. His discussion of the peopling of the earth comes in the *Antiquities of the Jews*, which appeared about A.D. 93. We read as follows[2]:

Japheth, son of Noah, had seven sons. These, beginning by inhabiting the mountains of Tauros and Amanus, advanced in Asia up to the river Tanais and in Europe as far as Gadeira, occupying the territory upon which they lit, and, as no inhabitant had preceded them, giving their own names to the nations. . . .

The children of Ham held the countries branching from Syria and the mountain-ranges of Amanus and Libanus, occupying all the district in the direction of the sea and appropriating the regions reaching to the ocean. . . .[3]

---

[1] The Authorized Version given above does not differ materially from the translation of St. Jerome.

[2] Trans. H. St. J. Thackeray, Loeb Library, iv. 59-71.

[3] In I. xv Josephus explains that 'Africa' derives its name from Apher, grandson to Abraham by Keturah's son Madan (the Epher of I Chron. i. 33): Thackeray, pp. 117-9.

Shem, the third of Noah's sons, had five sons, who inhabited Asia as far as the Indian Ocean, beginning at the Euphrates.

Here, it will be noticed, there is no simple equation of the continents with the three sons of Noah, but Japheth's progeny are broadly allocated to Europe, Ham's to Africa and Shem's to the East. Josephus thus more or less adheres to the scriptures[1] and his inventive mind is directed—in passages not reproduced above—to an elaborate identification of the names of the grandchildren of Noah with names of races in his own day, an exercise which was to be repeatedly copied and extended in the centuries ahead.

The lead given by Josephus does not seem to have been followed by other writers for long enough. Even as late as the early fifth century the Spanish Christian Orosius in his careful *History* does not deal with the matter. He touches on the flood—but only to moralize[2]; and he gives a full recapitulation of the geographical division into three continents which was to form the basis of nearly every subsequent Christian account[3] yet he does not link the sons of Noah with the tripartite *orbis*. His own master Augustine was to take the discussion a great deal further and, as was his manner, to enrich it with all sorts of original reflections.

That the matter was treated by St. Augustine incidentally is beside the point. Thus the tripartite world is treated in one section of the *City of God* and the generations of Noah in another: but both were clearly linked. Here is his description of the continents—appended as a gloss on account of the conquest of Asia by Ninus, son of Belus, who was descended from Shem's son Asshur.[4]

Here by Asia I mean not that region which is a single province of greater Asia but the entire area which is so called. Some regard it as

---

[1] He improves on the order of Genesis by treating the Tower of Babel *before* dealing with the diffusion of the races.

[2] *Adversus paganos historiarum lib. vii*, I. iii.

[3] *Ibid.*, I. ii: it is a measure of his care that he here records that for some there are only two continents—Europe and Africa being taken together.

[4] *De Civ. Dei*, XVI. iii.

one of two parts, but most as a third of the whole world—Asia, Europe and Africa would thus comprise the whole. But the divisions are not equal. For the part termed Asia goes from the South through the East to the North; Europe, however, from the North to the West and Africa thence from the West to the South. So we see that half the world contains two parts, Europe and Africa, and the other half only one, Asia. These two parts arise because all the water that flows between the lands comes in between them from the Ocean, forming the Mediterranean. So that if you divide the inhabited world into two, an eastern and a western half, Asia will be in the one, Europe and Africa in the other.[1]

This was to be almost the last occasion on which a plain halving of the world is taken seriously; its implausibility is inherent in this passage.

St. Augustine's reflections on the inheritances of Noah's sons are scattered through chapters devoted to a commentary on the period of Jewish history from the Flood to the time of Abraham. The interpretative method of St. Augustine is fully stretched:

We investigate these secrets of divine scripture as best we may, some in greater and some in less harmony with the truth, but holding it a matter of faith that these things have not been done and written without some foreshadowing of future events and are to be related only to Christ and His church, which is the City of God.[2]

The starting point is a consideration of the meaning of the Hebrew names: Shem is 'interpreted' as 'named'; Japheth is 'breadth' (enlargement); Ham is 'hot'.[3] Shem is

---

[1] Ed. Dombart, (Teubner) XVI. xvii (ii. 154): Asiam nunc dico non illam partem quae huius maioris Asiae una provincia est, sed eam quae universa Asia nuncupatur, quam quidam in altera duarum, plerique autem in tertia totius orbis parte posuerunt, ut sint omnes Asia, Europa, et Africa; quod non aequali divisione fecerunt. Namque ista, quae Asia nuncupatur, a meridie per orientem usque ad septentrionem pervenit; Europa vero a septentrione usque ad occidentem, atque inde Africa ab occidente usque ad meridiem. Unde videntur orbem dimidium duae tenere, Europa et Africa, alium vero dimidium sola Asia. Sed ideo illae duae partes factae sunt, quia inter utramque ab Oceano ingreditur, quidquid aquarum terras interluit; et hoc mare magnum nobis facit. Quapropter si in duas partes orbem dividas Orientis et Occidentis, Asia erit in una, in altera vero Europa et Africa.

[2] XVI. ii (ii. 124): 'Haec scripturae secreta divinae indagamus, ut possumus, alius alio magis minusve congruenter, verum tamen fideliter certum tenentes non ea sine aliqua praefiguratione futurorum gesta atque conscripta neque nisi ad Christum et eius ecclesiam, quae civitas Dei est, esse referenda.'

[3] *Loc. cit.* (ii. 122): 'nominatus ... latitudo ... calidus'.

'named' because of his seed was to come the humanity of
Christ. Japheth is 'enlarged', appropriately because, as
we read in Genesis ix. 27, 'God shall enlarge Japheth and
he shall dwell in the tents of Shem'. And as for Ham, 'he
surely signifies the hot brand of heretics, hot not in
wisdom but in wilfulness'.[1] The cursing of Canaan, son
of Ham, had already attracted the attention of Lactantius,
who traced to it the origin of astrology and false religion.[2]
St. Augustine took the matter further and a further step
was taken in the establishment of that fearful tradition
which was sometimes to justify in later ages an attitude
to the African negroes which precluded them from a full
enjoyment of the Christian revelation.

> As for Shem and Japheth, they stand respectively for circumcision
> and uncircumcision, or as the apostle put it in another way, for Jews
> and Greeks, those who are called and justified.[3]

No one influenced speculation in later centuries more
than St. Augustine. Yet his contemporary St. Jerome,
while not so great a theologian or philosopher, was in his
way as potent a force. His Latin version of the Bible was
to be the greatest single work of literature in the post-
Roman world and besides moulding the sentiments of
later ages in this way, he also composed commentaries
on much of the Bible which were to be frequently copied
and elaborated by later writers. His notes on chapters 9
and 10 of Genesis[4] summarize the views of earlier writers.
Shem is the originator of the Jews, Japheth of the Gentiles.
Shem's generations populated Asia, less the fraction which
went with Japheth's children to Europe; and Ham's sons
had the whole continent of Africa ('una climatis pars').
The only novel contribution of St. Jerome was his gloss
on the passage describing the 'enlargement' of Japheth

[1] 'Quid significat nisi haereticorum genus calidum, non spiritu sapientiae'
sed inpatientiae?'

[2] *Divinae Institutiones*, ii. ch. 14; P.L. 6, cols. 327-9.

[3] *De Civ. Dei*, ii. 122-3: 'Sem vero et Iapheth tamquam circumcisio et
praeputium, vel sicut alio modo eos appellat apostolus, Iudaei et Graeci, sed
vocati et iustificati.' The reference is to Galatians ii. 7-9.

[4] *Quaestiones in Genesim*, P.L. 23, cols. 998-1004.

and his dwelling in the tents of Shem. This St. Jerome took to refer to the Christians' monopoly of scholarship and scriptural knowledge, the earlier monopoly of the Jews having been overthrown.[1]

The ensuing centuries elaborated these themes. St. Eucher, bishop of Lyons in the middle of the fifth century, besides repeating the remarks of St. Jerome on the Christians evicting the Jews as custodians of God and Wisdom, summarises the continental pattern which we have been examining:

> We must observe that the three sons of Noah after the Flood occupied the three parts of the world. For the posterity of Shem extended over Asia, or the East, the posterity of Ham Africa or the South, and Japheth Europe, with part of Asia and the West.[2]

And a century later the eccentric Egyptian Christian, Cosmas Indicopleustes, was so confident of this arrangement that he accused the pagans of 'availing themselves of what Moses' (he means Genesis) 'had revealed' and dividing 'the whole earth into three parts: Asia, Libya and Europe'.[3] This, indeed, was to turn the tables and claim the three fold division of the world as originating, not with the Greeks, but with the Jews. Certainly it shows how necessary to the divine dispensation a tripartite division was felt to be.

The traditions of late antiquity, both classical and patristic, are gathered together in the *Etymologies* of Isidore of Seville, who died in 636. A very full description of the tripartite world is given ('divisus est trifarie') out of Solinus, Orosius and Jerome; there is a reference to the twofold division and a paraphrase of St. Augustine's

---

[1] *Loc. cit.*—'de nobis prophetatur, qui in eruditione et scientia scripturarum, ejecto Israele, versamur'.

[2] 'Notandum vero est, tres Noe filios, tres post diluvium terrae partes occupasse. Sem namque posteritas in Asiam vel Orientem, Cham in Africam vel Meridiem, Japheth cum parte Asiae in Europam se Occidentemque porrexerunt.' P.L. 50, col. 777; cf. *ibid.* 937-8.

[3] *Christian Topography*, trans. and ed. J. W. McCrindle, Hakluyt Society 1897, p. 37; the limits of the threefold division are given in some detail on pp. 33-5. Cosmas may have been a Nestorian: intro., p. ix.

remarks on this.[1] The allocation of the sons of Noah to the world thus divided is found in a long section in which the names of the generations of each of Noah's sons is related to the names of later peoples—a preoccupation which, as we have seen, goes back to Josephus.[2] The only real novelty in Isidore's treatment of these matters is in his glosses on the meaning of the names of Ham and Japheth. Ham, he says, presages the future, because his descendants were to dwell in a part of the earth which, since it was nearer the sun, was hotter than elsewhere.[3] This idea was to be worked out later. As for Japheth, we are to suppose that 'enlargement' means the multiplication of the faithful[4] and the interpretation takes a step towards the literal victory of Japheth's children over Shem's which was to be a popular view in the middle ages.[5]

By the seventh century of our era we therefore have all the ingredients of an attitude to the continents which might have filled them with the emotional content which they lacked in the pagan period. Europe was the land of Japheth, of the Gentiles, the Greeks and the Christians; Asia was the land of Semitic peoples, glorious in that they had produced the patriarchs and prophets, the chosen people and Christ himself; but—as the land of the circumcised adherents of older laws—condemned to an inferiority which was stated in the scriptures: 'God shall enlarge Japheth and he shall dwell in the tents of Shem.' As for Africa, the lot of the unhappy descendants of Ham, the Hamitic subjection was equally clearly laid down: Canaan was to be the servant both of Shem and Japheth:

[1] *Etymologiarum sive Originum libri XX*, ed. W. M. Lindsay, XIV. ii; book XIV as a whole deals with the world and its parts.

[2] IX. ii.

[3] VII. vi. 17: 'Cham calidus, et ipse ex praesagio futuri cognominatus, Posteritas enim eius eam terrae partem possedit, quae vicino sole calentior est.'

[4] VII. vi. 18: 'Ex eo enim populus gentium nascitur; et quia lata est ex gentibus multitudo credentium, ab eadem latitudine Iapheth dictus est.'

[5] We may note also that Isidore treated the Europa story with scant respect, *ibid.* VIII. xi. 35-6: 'Iuppiter . . . fuit enim in navi cuius insigne erat taurus. . . . Et ideo non figurae istae sunt, sed plane de veritate scelera.' This was to be a standard gloss: cf. Boccaccio, *De genealogia deorum*, II, cap. lxii.

'a servant of servants shall he be unto his brethren.'
What was to result from this marriage of Europa and
Japheth?

CHAPTER 2

CHRISTENDOM

As the fabric of Roman hegemony crumbled, an era of Mediterranean empires was closed. The intellectual, commercial and political domination of the Greeks had produced in the end the Macedonian empire, straddling three continents. This in turn was followed by the rise of Rome. The masters of Italy became the conquerors of the Hellenistic east, of North Africa, of western Europe. Their empire was supracontinental. It did not coincide with the whole of any one continent (for despite the conquest of Gaul and Britain, the whole of central and northern Europe lay beyond the Roman frontier) but covered portions of all three, which were bound to each other and to Rome by the routes of the inland sea and a network of military roads. Long before the final collapse these links were growing tenuous. Few Roman soldiers marched along the roads of the Empire in the fourth century and the Syrian and Jewish mariners who fetched and carried at sea for their Roman employers and customers did less business than before. The empire was officially divided and subdivided in an effort to make government more efficient by decentralization, to match with administrative devolution the increasing social and economic autonomy of the provinces. To these developments the barbarian penetration merely added the *coup de grâce*. Most of the world that had been Rome was from the fifth century divided into a multiplicity of small states. In the east, it is true, a great fragment of the Empire survived based on Constantinople and with provinces in Europe, in Asia Minor and in Africa. Justinian in the mid-sixth century ruled over the Balkans south of the

Danube, over the Nile valley and Cyrenaica in Africa, and Asia Minor up to Persia. He added to these by the conquest of Carthage, of the south-east of Visigothic Spain, and of Ostrogothic Italy. But these acquisitions were short-lived. Before long the boundary of the Greek Empire was contracting. Later emperors had a hard job of it to retain control of their Balkan lands, the Greek islands and Anatolia, though Constantinople remained for long the centre of a state greater than any in the west.

There the division of political power was carried to its logical conclusion. A multiplicity of German tribes straggled over into Britain, Gaul, Spain and Italy and petty kings, ineffectually aping Rome, established themselves and their followers in the provinces of the empire. In much that was important—religion, language, literature—the German invaders were as much victims as victors, but political unity was abolished. How could it survive in a time when the possession of land meant power, when the notions of administration, of taxation, of bureaucracy were dying? The war-band and its leader was the unit of political power, and on a territorial basis the land was divided among magnates whose fortified dwellings were immune from the control of all but a more powerful chieftain. Loyalty and service were enforced not by public sanctions but by the bonds of kinship and the vendetta. Custom replaced written law. No larger allegiances were conceivable than the respect paid to the mysterious ancestry of a tribal king, though the growing use of land as a reward for military support invested the ambitious and successful leader with at any rate the beginnings of a more practical authority.

Yet the very absence of effective political controls permitted the transmission of older ideas about the world and the growth of new ideas among the Christian clergy. The invading Germans were either pagans or else Arian Christians, disciples of a version of Christianity which had penetrated into northern Europe in the fifth century. As they advanced into the provinces of the empire the Germans encountered a Christian church, especially strong in the towns, with a relatively well-educated and well-born episcopate and a habit of looking to Rome and its bishops for guidance in organization and dogma, not surprising in a church which had been practically adopted by the state in the later Empire. The nearer the Germans got to the Mediterranean the stronger they found the Roman church and, if the fragile Christianity of Britain was overwhelmed and driven into the Celtic highlands, elsewhere the barbarians ultimately accepted Latin Christianity, abandoning either their Arianism or their paganism. These 'conversions' proceeded usually from the top downwards. A king was baptised and then his people followed. Such proselytizing was often skin-deep, no doubt; relapses were common enough; a tough strain of barbaric 'superstition' survived for centuries, even if driven underground. But the conversion of the Germanic peoples is nevertheless of fundamental importance for our story, for it provided at each stage the framework of a society larger than tribe or petty kingdom.[1]

How greatly the new religion was the plaything of kings is to be seen in the paradoxical situation where a ruthless Frankish adventurer, Clovis king of Tournai, could adopt Latin Christianity and enforce it in Gaul long before the church of Rome was undisputed master of Italy itself; in Italy for a long time royal support was given—by Ostrogoths as later by Lombards—to Arianism. In Spain, too, politics determined the fate of religion and dissident magnates cultivated Arianism in the face of kings professing Latin Christianity. Thus outside Gaul (where the only rival to the Latin church besides the pagan pantheon was the Celtic church in Brittany) the western provinces of the old Empire saw two churches

[1] For what follows see Kenneth Scott Latourette, *A history of the Expansion of Christianity*: ii, *The Thousand Years of Uncertainty*, London 1939, with abundant bibliographies.

more or less side by side in the sixth and seventh centuries. But if there were two churches, there was only one hierarchy and it was to the possession of this that the Roman church owed the friendship of kings and its ability to withstand Arian attack. By about 700 the communities obedient to Rome were entirely in the ascendant in Italy as well as in Gaul, and Arianism in Spain was about to be engulfed in common disaster with the Latin faith by the advance of the Moslems.

Elsewhere in Europe the process of conversion was equally slow and unsure. In Britain the united efforts of Celtic and Roman missionaries ensured a more or less Christian England by early in the seventh century, but in both Britain and France the Danish invasions produced a setback and it is only by the start of the tenth century that the Danelaw in England and Normandy in France were again Christian. Frisia, Bavaria, Hesse and Saxony were the scene of prolonged evangelical effort culminating in Charlemagne's forcible conversion of the Saxon leader Widukind in 785; but the conversion of Scandinavia was not accomplished till the eleventh and twelfth centuries. The Slav lands of north and central Europe were converted by a similar combination of moral persuasion and war. Bohemia, Poland and the Wend lands of north Germany were converted more than once from the ninth century onwards but were only really absorbed into Christianity by the twelfth century. Even as late as the thirteenth century large areas of northern Europe were overtly pagan and in the Wendish areas and in Pomerania it was settlement by Germans which made Christianity something more than a superficial conversion.

The spreading of the Christian faith summarized above was the work of the Latin church, the papacy playing a considerable part in the process in and after the pontificate of Gregory the Great. The achievements of the eastern Greek church centred on Constantinople were less sustained but are none the less important in our story. The

Balkan peoples received missionaries from the Greek church and by the end of the ninth century Serbs and Bulgars were more or less Christian, there being some competition for control between the Byzantine patriarch and the Roman pope. A century later the Russians of Kiev and Novgorod had accepted Greek Christianity, though—like the Bulgars—they finally rejected the hegemony of the patriarch of Constantinople. As for Christianity in the Asiatic and North African territories of the Eastern Empire, it was during the sixth century that the Middle East and beyond saw the penetration of scattered groups of Christians disowned alike by Rome and Constantinople—Monophysites in the Nile valley and Ethiopia, Nestorians and Jacobites in Persia, central Asia and the Orient. These groups were small and usually ill-organized, a minority existing on sufferance. Their mere existence, however, was to affect the development of the notion of Christian unity in the predominantly Christian West. Nor must it be forgotten that the emperors at Constantinople were always profoundly conscious of their mission as leaders of the Christian *oecumene*.

Thus as against the disintegration of the state in the area where Rome had once been supreme, we must set the gradual unification accomplished in the field of religion. Admittedly the Christianization we have outlined was accomplished painfully slowly and formed for long a mere official covering over habits of mind which were essentially pagan. Admittedly there were differences between one sort of Christianity and another, some of which (like those between the Celtic and Roman churches) time smoothed out and others (like those between the Greek and Roman churches) which time deepened and intensified. Yet by the thirteenth century the cross was a universal symbol from the Black Sea to the Atlantic and from the Mediterranean to the Arctic Circle. To the east a fringe of eccentric churches was a vague memory of an even more oecumenical purpose.

PLATE II. Part of a fifteenth-century portolan from Nordenskiöld, *Periplus*. See p. 94 and n. 1.

Much, of course, survived from Rome that was to be valuable in the flux of the dark ages. If land and power were severely localized, the clergy had longer memories than the laity, a tenaciously held grip on literature and a respect for older ways of political thought. The idea of empire scarcely died out even in the West, if only because the emperor at Constantinople was a direct inheritor of Rome. Charlemagne in 800 became emperor in the West and thereafter the notion of empire had its practical as well as its nostalgic aspects for this area. Among a handful of scholars the geographical science of antiquity was still recalled. And there was even a lingering acknowledgement of the old dividing line between barbarism and civilization. All these notions came to colour the medieval picture of society, but were in every sense subsidiary to the developing sense of unity based on the church, the notion that the final division in the world was between Christians and the rest.

This concept was by no means a simple territorial antithesis. The early church had been a scattered and often persecuted minority of elect. To choose the faith involved a conscious abnegation of the world and long after the explicit adoption of Christianity as an official cult this earlier view of renunciation was given classical expression by St. Augustine. In the *City of God* he taught that the church was distinct in principle from the things of the world, that society was a product of man's sin, that life here below was militant exile. The converse of such an attitude was the view that Christianity was not tied to any narrow man-made frontiers, and had no boundaries in time or space. Yet already in Augustine's day and rapidly thereafter a hierarchy developed which gave concrete territorial expression to religious units. Some states were Christian, some were not. Some parts of the world were organized in the service of the Church, other parts were hostile or indifferent. A variety of particular and

c

tangible churches existed alongside of the transcendental Church.

How profoundly these ambiguities penetrated into the consciousness of the West may be seen in the equivocal vocabulary of the vernaculars. The two Latin words for the faith and the sum of its practitioners only settled down by the ninth century as *christianismus* (the faith) and *christianitas* (the faithful).[1] And a wide variety of derivative words suggests the uncertainty referred to. In Italian, French and Spanish it was *christianitas* (*cristianità*, *chrétienté*, *cristianidad*) which emerged as the term for what Englishmen in general called Christendom; but there are hints of both a Latin and a vernacular development of *christianismus* in exactly the same direction—as when a fifteenth-century clerk in England describes Henry IV as 'miles laudatissimus, Christianismo et Paganismo peroptime probatus' and a contemporary Italian writer says Italy is 'the worthiest and most noble portion of all *cristianesimo*'.[2] In German *das Christentum*, the exact etymological equivalent of English 'Christendom', gained in the middle ages acceptance in the sense of the religion and *die Christenheit* as the equivalent of *christianitas*.[3] In middle English—and indeed later—'Christianity' can, however, still be found as equivalent of Christendom, as well as of the religion itself.

> 'O tell me, tell me, Tam', she says,
> 'For his sake that died on tree,
> If ye were ever in holy chapel,
> Or sain'd in Christentie.'

[1] See *Thesaurus* for early examples of the abstraction, not yet in the sense of Christendom and cf. below, pp. 27-8.

[2] J. Rous, *Historia Regum Angliae*, ed. Hearne, 1745, p. 206; Giovanni Rucellai, *Zibaldone* (1466) quoted by W. H. Woodward, *Education during the Renaissance* (1906), p. 78: 'Italia, la quale è la più degna e più nobile parte di tutto il cristianesimo'; Florence 'la quale è reputata la più degna e la più bella patria che abbi non tanto il cristianesimo ma tutto l'universo mondo'. It is possible that we have here the influence of Greek Χριστιανισμός, which had the sense of Christendom, but there are other Italian examples.

[3] The locus classicus of German usage in the early thirteenth century is Walther von der Vogelweide, *Leich*: 'Unkristenlicher dinge ist al diu Kristenheit sô vol', etc., 1. 630f. I owe this information to Mr. W. L. Wardale.

Here we have the sense which was to last. But here we have a totally different use:

> He is either himsell a devil frae hell
> Or else his mother a witch maun be;
> I wadna have ridden that wan water
> For a' the gowd in Christentie.

'Christianity' in the sense of 'Christendom' in English usage was doubtless a result of French influence.[1]

Whatever lingering confusions these linguistic variations imply, the hardening of the division between Christians and their lands and the non-Christian world went on apace. The antithesis between barbarism and civilization nevertheless had an astonishingly long life. The fathers of the church, imbued with Roman values, for the most part regarded Christianized Rome and civilization as interchangeable terms and such an attitude is also found sometimes even in St. Augustine, faced as he was with the threat of Vandals and other savage invaders who were enemies of both church and empire. Gregory the Great can still distinguish barbarian kings from Roman emperors in terms of the freedom of their subjects—much as Herodotus and other Greeks had distinguished Persians from Greeks. Such identifications were, of course, implicit in the close connection between the Roman Empire and the Christian Church. To be a Christian after Constantine was to be a Roman. Such categories naturally became less meaningful as barbarians became Christian. Einhard opposes barbarians and Latins only on the level of grammar and pronunciation. The terms 'barbarian' and 'barbarous' tended to have a meaning in literature rather than politics during the eleventh and twelfth centuries. When we do (on rare occasions) meet the terms in a political sense it is significant that 'Christian' and 'barbarian' can be opposed to one another as in a charter

---

[1] The two ballads are 'Tam Lin' and 'Kinmont Willie'. A fourteenth-century occurrence of Christianity=Christendom will be found in *Cursor Mundi*, ed. R. Morris, (E.E.T.S. 1874), i. 130. Cf. further *O.E.D.*

of Otto III to the merchants of Magdeburg in which they are privileged to trade in his kingdom 'not only in Christian but also in barbarian areas'. It is significant in this connection that Moslems were firmly regarded as idolatrous pagans, worshipping Mahomet, who was the embodiment of evil. As a picture of Islam and its somewhat puritanical values this had not even the verisimilitude of a caricature, but it fitted in with a necessary view of the non-Christian world.[1] Roger Bacon, to whom the antithesis of barbarism and rationality was meaningful,[2] was almost alone in crediting some pagans—despite their spiritual inferiority—with superiority to Christians 'in those virtues which conduce to human decency, social activity and intercourse'.[3]

Nothing, it may be suspected, did more to compel a specifically territorial view of Christianity than the vigour and success of Moslem attacks during the three hundred years that lay between the death of the Prophet in 632 and the break-up of the united Caliphate in the ninth and tenth centuries. For this there were three reasons: the danger of engulfment which made Christians in the west forget minor differences; the policy of Islam to Christian

[1] In the *Enciclopedia Italiana*, s.v. 'Barbari' will be found a short but useful discussion of medieval attitudes (including the quotation of Otto III's charter). In opposition to the point of view taken by the writer of this article, Rodolfo de Mattei has written a valuable short study 'Sul concetto di barbaro e barbarie nel medio evo', *Studi di storia e diritto in onore di Enrico Besta*, vol. iv (Milan 1939), 483-501. This argues that the Roman viewpoint (that *Latinitas* and *barbaries* were opposed terms) survived virtually unbroken throughout the medieval period. He adduces, however, no evidence between the patristic and early dark ages on the one hand, and the fourteenth century on the other, and fails adequately to discuss the association between Christianity and Rome, with all its important consequences. Much clearly remains to be found out about barbarism as a category in the eleventh to thirteenth centuries (cf. next note for a thirteenth-century example). On the attitude of the Fathers see also J. R. Palanque, *Saint Ambroise et l'Empire Romain*, Paris 1933, pp. 325-35. On barbarism as a literary term see E. R. Curtius, *European Literature and the Latin Middle Ages*, London 1953, p. 44.

[2] '. . . regiones barbarorum, regiones hominum rationabilium', *Opus Majus*, ed. J. H. Bridges, 3 vols., Oxford 1897-1900, i. 301.

[3] '. . . in virtutibus quae communiter requiruntur ad vitae honestatem et ad communionem humanae societatis, et sermonem, sumus eis [paganis] impares et operibus minus efficaces', *ibid.*, ii. 322-3.

minorities within its own frontiers; and the bitter hostility
and contempt of Arabs for their enemies. Each of these
aspects of Islamic-Christian contact acted upon the in-
cipient sense of unity in the west.

The danger was very great. The seventh century saw
the Arabs masters of Syria, Palestine, Egypt and the North
African coast; in the eighth century the Arabs were at the
gate of Constantinople and, after conquering Spain, penetrated into southern France; in the ninth century Rome
was sacked in 846 and the Saracens obtained not only
Sicily but temporary footholds in the mainland of southern Italy. From our point of view the contemporary
alarm and its significance for the emergence of a sense of
unity can be seen in the invention by the eighth century
chronicler Isidor Pacensis of a term to describe the composite forces—Romano-Gallic and barbarian—which
under the leadership of the Frankish chief Charles Martel
defeated the Moslems at the battle of Tours in 732: he
calls them 'Europeans'—*Europeenses*.[1]

Not only did lands in Europe fall to the Moslem invaders, not only did Jerusalem itself become part of their
empire, but the general diffusion of Christianity in Asia
and Africa was imperilled. The remoter Nestorian and
Jacobite churches were cut off by the Saracen occupation
of much of Asia Minor and then of Persia; the Abyssinian
church was likewise isolated. And, subjected to a combination of contemptuous toleration and discriminatory
taxation, the Christians under Arab rule declined severely
in numbers and conviction. Surviving Christian communities in Egypt and Syria were soon relatively uninfluential and developed doctrinally even further from
Roman and Greek orthodoxy. If the Christians of Europe
were compelled at times to recognize their community as

[1] 'Prospiciunt Europeenses Arabum tentoria ordinata', P.L. 96, col. 8271,
quoted H. F. Muller, *A Chronology of Vulgar Latin*, Halle 1929, p. 46; I owe the
reference to Professor M. Sandmann. Cf. Mare Bloch. *Société féodale*, i (1939),
p. 6 and note.

such, the Christians of Asia and Africa were gradually isolated and reduced to insignificance.[1]

The Islamic tolerance of the Christian and Jewish minorities within Moslem areas was accompanied by the practice of holy war by the Arabs. For them the world was divided into Dar al-Islam, the abode of submission to God, and Dar al-Harb, the abode of war. 'Unlike Christianity, which preached a peace that it never achieved, Islam unashamedly came with a sword.'[2] If Christians were committed to ways of peace (and the orthodox Greek Church seems to have taken this more seriously than the Roman Church),[3] they could scarcely avoid glorifying a war which was not only waged for self-preservation but which aimed at preserving and even extending the faith. Soon the sense of inevitable opposition was shared by western soldiers as well as Arabs, and the eleventh century heard the bard of the *Song of Roland* proclaim the distinction as axiomatic:

Pagans are wrong and Christians right.[4]

Holy war on the limits of Christendom, the Crusade, was to be a permanent feature of Christian activity from the eleventh century onwards.

Such a view of the political obligations of Christian society would probably not have developed rapidly in the eleventh century if the reduction in the area of Christian obedience had not then been accompanied by changes in the world of Islam. These went far to severing the links with Jerusalem maintained by Christians through the tolerance previously exercised by the Arab masters of Palestine. It was the irruption of the Seljuks which pro-

---

[1] W. H. C. Frend, 'North Africa and Europe in the early Middle Ages', *Trans. Roy. Hist. Soc.*, 5th Ser. v (1955), 61-80, gives an excellent description of the detachment of North Africa and Syria from Europe in the sphere of politics, economics and religion.

[2] S. Runciman, *A History of the Crusades: i. The First Crusade*, 1951, p. 15. See, too, *Encyclopaedia of Islam*, s.vv. 'Dar al Islam', 'Dar al Harib'. I have profited from discussing these Islamic concepts with Dr. Norman Daniel.

[3] *Ibid.*, p. 83-4.

[4] *Chanson de Roland*, v. 1015: 'Paien unt tort e chrestiens unt dreit.'

voked the first crusade, but before we proceed to a consideration of the dynamic expansion of Christendom, we must pause to consider what at this time the notion of Christendom involved.

The universal mission of Christianity is the basis of the medieval notion of Christendom: the practical disposal of Christians on the surface of the earth gave frontiers to what was oecumenical by definition. That Christ came to save *all* men is evident throughout the New Testament, and is elaborated most fully in the gospel of St. John:

> The same came for a witness, to bear witness of the Light, that all men through him might believe. (i. 7)
> And I, if I be lifted up from the earth, will draw all men unto me.
> (xii. 32)

These words are echoed and made more precise in the Pauline epistles at many points but especially by the catalogue in Colossians iii. 11:

> where there is neither Greek nor Jew, circumcision nor uncircumcision, Barbarian, Scythian, bond nor free: but Christ is all and in all.

Yet, as we have seen, the spreading of Christianity was uneven. At first it radiated out from its east Mediterranean birthplace, covering the Hellenistic east and Romanized North Africa and Europe. But soon the conversion of Asia and Africa was halted, the adoption of Christianity in Europe proceeded slowly and thus a boundary existed to the region which could be termed Christian. The term 'Christianitas'—Christendom—was ultimately used to describe this area.

The evolution of the notion of Christendom was as leisurely, as full of moments of retreat and confusion, as the advance of the religion itself.[1] An abstract term for all the faithful, distinct from the word 'ecclesia' (church)

---

[1] Jean Rupp, *L'idée de Chrétienté dans la pensée pontificale des origines à Innocent III*, Paris 1939, surveys the evidence up to the beginning of the thirteenth century as far as it is given in papal correspondence; cf. also *Dictionnaire de Théologie Catholique*, tables générales, s.v. 'Chrétienté'. Despite its title there is nothing useful for the present subject in B. Landry, *L'Idée de Chrétienté chez les scolastiques du XIII siècle*, Paris 1929.

with its tendency towards a narrower meaning (the clergy, the hierarchy) was an obvious linguistic necessity and in Greek Χριστιανισμός was an early candidate.[1] The Latin equivalent (Christianismus) was, however, patently a Grecism and, as we have seen, came to mean primarily the religion and not its adherents.[2] A good Latin abstraction, Christianitas, also appears in the patristic period though at first its social sense was vague—it meant all the faithful, certainly, but in a transcendental sense, devoid for long of political overtones. This did not mean that the notion of social and political coherence between all members of the religion was absent; only that a fixed terminology had not emerged. Men used 'Christiani', 'Christians', in such a way, and (more explicitly) 'Christianorum genus' or 'populus Christianus'. St. Augustine (and after him Gregory the Great) used 'Christiana respublica' with a similar sense, though here the association is with the Roman empire, which also clearly suggested the employment of terms such as 'Christianum imperium' and 'Christianus orbis'.[3] It is instructive to witness the efforts of Bede, writing as late as the early decades of the eighth century, to secure the expression of a concept which might in a rough and ready way be translated as 'Christendom' without having the word at his disposal. He describes Gregory the Great as being pope 'over the whole world', and being set over 'all the churches which obey the true faith'.[4] Faced with exactly the same linguistic problem a century earlier, St. Columba had even addressed the pope as 'Head of all the churches of the whole of Europe'.[5]

[1] Rupp, p. 9, cites a use by St. Ignatius of Antioch which he considers bears this meaning.

[2] See above, p. 22 and refs.

[3] For a discussion of these terms see Rupp, pp. 25-33.

[4] *Opera historica*, ed. King (Loeb), i. 184 (ii. cap. 1): Quia cum primum in toto orbe pontificatum gereret, et conversis iamdudum ad fidem veritatis esset praelatus ecclesiis, nostram gentem eatenus idolis mancipatam, Christi fecit ecclesiam.

[5] Sancti Columbani *Opera*, ed. and trans. G. S. M. Walker, Dublin 1957, p. 36.

Christendom is thus at first a floating concept, as insecure as the religion whose totality it sought to describe, and it is not till the ninth century that the term 'Christianitas' emerges in the writings of popes Nicholas I (858-67) and John VIII (872-82) with a harder, more deliberate meaning.[1] As used by John VIII in particular 'Christianitas' is sharply distinguished from 'ecclesia' and it is significant that it is adopted especially with reference to Saracen danger in expressions like 'defensio Christianitatis'.[2] Others at this time were also groping towards a view of society which was in conformity with this. Hincmar of Rheims, for instance, can write of the 'one kingdom and the unity of the church' as practically synonymous terms.[3] The papacy, however, with its necessarily larger view of the pressures on the church as a whole, had a clearer inducement to fill *Christianitas* with new meaning. Yet John VIII's Christendom is still without frontiers and we must wait until the pontificate of Gregory VII (1073-85) for a physical or geographical connotation. The word is not frequently found in his correspondence, but when we do encounter it, it has a corporate reality which leaves no doubt of its sense: 'fines Christianitatis', the boundaries of Christendom, occurs; the pope states that the Roman church is 'magistra totius Christianitatis'; the term 'Christianitas' includes people, kings and clergy, viewed as one unit.[4] The ground is thus prepared for the extension of the idea accomplished at the time of the first Crusade and in the pontificate of Urban II (1088-99).

The correspondence of Urban II yields few examples of 'Christianitas' but there is no doubt of the influence exerted on the concept by the address he gave at the

---

[1] Rupp, p. 18. [2] *Ibid.*, 35-52.
[3] 'Nec dici debet, ut inter principes nostros de una gente vel de uno regno, ad aliam gentem vel ad aliud regnum quisque refugiat, sed potius in uno regno sicut Christianos decet, et in unitate Ecclesiae matris consistant', *De divortio Lotharii et Tetbirgae*, P.L., 125, col. 699; cf. cols. 746-7.
[4] Rupp, 53-71.

Council of Clermont, which was to launch the first Crusade. That we can have no firm knowledge of what exactly Urban said at Clermont in 1095 need not bother us unduly, for the speeches put into his mouth by chroniclers in the ensuing decades without doubt represent the general tenor of his words and, even more significant for our purpose, the sense of contemporaries as to what it was reasonably proper for the pope to have said at this moment of crisis.[1] The crisis was the greatest experienced by Christians since the first wave of Saracen attacks. The Seljuk Turks, at first mere mercenaries of the Arabs, had seized power in Egypt and then proceeded to absorb Asia Minor. They were a race of Tartar origin and their adoption of Islam did not give them the sense of mission, centralised and directed to systematic expansion, which had characterised the first Islamic empire: they were adventurers led by adventurers. The provinces of the Greek empire were threatened by war bands and Jerusalem, centre of the world, in their hands (1071) was both less accessible to pilgrims than it had been under the looser control of the Arabs and a symbol of the threat to the whole Christian community.

It is not that the reporters of Urban's speech use the term *Christianitas* in its full meaning as Christendom, for they do so only in a very incidental way.[2] What makes their words important is that they are imbued with a sense of Christendom. There is first of all a unanimous acceptance of the global mission of Christianity and an acceptance of the Greek Church as part of the community of Christians. There is also an assumption of the territorial nature of the church viewed in this social way and

[1] Most of the texts of the various versions of the sermon are conveniently assembled in P.L. 151, cols. 565-82 and all are discussed by Dana C. Munro ('The Speech of Pope Urban II at Clermont, 1095', *American Hist. Review*, xi (1906), pp. 231-42), in an attempt to establish the substance of the pope's remarks by abstracting what is common to the earliest accounts.

[2] Guibert of Nogent, indeed, used the word rather in its transcendental or religious sense: 'cultum Christianitatis', 'ubi nunc paganismus est, Christianitas fiat', 'Christianitatis imperium'; P.L. 151, col. 578.

a conviction that the brotherhood of all Christians has a political aspect no less than a sacramental. The Turkish threat had forced an awareness on Christendom of the common elements in its various component parts.

The best account of Urban's speech from this point of view is that given by the English chronicler William of Malmesbury. After attributing the disaster to God's punishment for human wickedness, the pope is made to point out that his hearers may recover grace by fighting for the cross[1]:

Therefore go forward in happiness and in confidence to attack the enemies of God. For these enemies (it should shame Christians to remember) have already occupied Syria, Armenia and latterly the whole of Asia Minor (whose provinces are Bithynia, Phrygia, Galatia, Lydia, Caria, Pamphylia, Isauria, Lycia, Cilicia). Now they traverse Illyria and all the land beyond as far as the Bosphorus. They have seized control of our Lord's sepulchre (unique pledge as it is of our faith) and make our pilgrims pay for permission to enter Jerusalem

[1] 'Ite ergo feliciter, ite confidenter, ad inimicos Dei persequendos. Illi enim jam pridem, proh! quantus Christianorum pudor! Syriam, Armeniam, omnem postremo Asiam Minorem, cujus provinciae sunt Bithinia, Frigia, Galatia, Lidia, Caria, Pamphilia, Isauria, Licia, Cilicia, occupaverunt; nunc Illiricum et omnes inferiores terras insolenter inequitant, usque ad mare quod Brachium Sancti Georgii vocatur. Quid quod Dominicum monumentum, unicum fidei pignus, ditioni suae vendicant, et ejus urbis introitum peregrinis nostris venditant, quae solis Christianis patere deberet, si aliquod solitae virtutis vestigium eis inesset: hoc, si solum esset, frontes nostras onerare sufficeret; jam vero quis ferat nisi multum iners, nisi Christianae gloriae invidus, quod non ex aequo divisimus orbem? Illi Asiam, tertiam mundi partem, ut haereditarium nidum inhabitant; quae a majoribus nostris aequa duabus residuis partibus, et tractuum longitudine, et provinciarum magnitudine, non immerito aestimata est. Ibi olim devotionis nostrae rami pillularunt, ibi apostoli omnes, praeter duos, mortes suas consecrarunt; ibi modo Christicolae, si qui supersunt, pauperculo agricolatu transigentes inediam, nefandis illis vectigal pensitant, vel tacitis suspiriis nostrae libertatis desiderantes conscientiam, quia perdidere suam. Illi Affricam, alteram orbis partem, ducentis jam annis et eo amplius armis possessam tenent; quod ideo Christiani honoris periculum pronuntio, quia fuerit terra illa olim praeclarorum ingeniorum altrix, quae divinis scriptis omnem vetustatis situm a se repellent quandiu fuerit qui Latinas litteras legat. Norunt litterati quod loquor. Tertium mundi clima restat Europa, cujus quantulam partem inhabitamus Christiani? nam omnem illam barbariem quae in remotis insulis glacialem frequentat oceanum, quia more belluino victitat, Christianam quis dixerit? Hanc igitur nostri mundi portiunculam Turci et Saraceni bello premunt; jamque a trecentis annis Hispania et Balearibus insulis subjugatis, quod reliquum est spe devorant, homines inertissimi, et qui, cominus pugandi fiduciam non habentes, fugax bellum diligunt.' William of Malmesbury, ed. W. Stubbs, R.S., ii, pp. 394-5.

which, had they a grain of their earlier humanity about them, should be open to Christians alone.

By itself this is enough to oppress our minds. But can any one with any initiative, anyone who cares for the glory of Christ, tolerate that we do not even share equally with them the inhabited earth? They have made Asia, which is a third of the world, their homeland —an area justly reckoned by our fathers as equal to the two other parts both for size and importance. There of old our religion first blossomed forth, and there all the apostles but two were martyred. Now the Christians there—if any survive—eke out a miserable living, pay taxes to their wicked masters and silently long to partake of our liberty having lost their own. They have also forcibly held Africa, the second portion of the world, for over two hundred years and I call this the ruin of Christian honour for this continent formerly nourished men of the greatest genius, whose inspired writings will ensure them immortality so long as there is anyone to cherish Latin literature: scholars will bear me out in this.

There remains Europe, the third continent. How small is the part of it inhabited by us Christians! for none would term Christian those barbarous people who live in distant islands on the frozen ocean, for they live in the manner of brutes. And even this fragment of our world is attacked by the Turks and Saracens. Three hundred years ago they conquered Spain and the Balearic Islands: now they covet the rest. But they are a singularly inactive lot, having little zest for warfare and preferring as they do a war when the enemy retreats.

William of Malmesbury explains the cowardly tactics of the Turks as a consequence of the climate in which they live: coming from a hot country they are more cunning than valorous. Here the Christian has a decided advantage.[1]

You are a people sprung from the more temperate regions of the world, and you lack neither martial prowess nor discretion: you are

[1] 'Vos estis gens quae in temperatioribus [Stubbs's *intemperatioribus* is surely an error] mundi provinciis oriunda; qui sitis et prodigi sanguinis ad mortis vulnerumque contemptum, et non careatis prudentia; namque et modestiam servatis in castris et in dimicatione utimini consiliis. Itaque, scientia et forti-tudine praediti, aggredimini memorabile iter, totis seculis praedicandi, si fratres vestros periculo exueritis. . . . Ituri et Christianitatem propugnaturi specimen crucis vestibus insigniant. . . . Cur ergo mortem timetis, qui sompni requiem, quae instar mortis est, diligitis? Res est nimirum dementiae, pro cupiditate brevis vitae, invidere sibi perpetuam. Quin potius, fratres charissimi, si ita contigerit, ponite pro fratribus animas vestras; vacuate ab impiis Dei sacrarium; extrudite latrones; inducite pios. Nulla vos necessitudinis pietas contineat, quia prima hominis pietas in Deum. Nullum natalis soli caritas tricet, quia diversis respectibus Christiano totus est mundus exilium et totus mundus patria; ita exilium patria, et patria exilium.' *Op. cit.*, pp. 396-8.

both disciplined in camp and skilful in the field of battle. Thus
endowed with wisdom and courage, you are embarking on a memor-
able enterprise. Your deeds will be sung down the ages if you rescue
your brothers from this danger.... May those who go forth as
champions of Christendom mark their clothes with the sign of the
cross.... Why fear death when you rejoice in the peace of sleep,
the pattern of death? It is surely insanity to endanger one's soul
through lust for a short space of living. Wherefore rather, my
dearest brothers, if it is necessary lay down your lives for your
brothers. Rid the sanctuary of God of the unbelievers, expel the
thieves and lead back the faithful. Let no loyalty to kinsfolk hold you
back; man's loyalty lies in the first place to God. No love of native
heath should delay you, for in one sense the whole world is exile for
a Christian, and in another the whole world is his country: so exile
is our fatherland, our fatherland exile.

The remarkable words in which William of Malmesbury gives the pope's message at the Council of Clermont
are worth pondering. We find in them traces of many of
the ideas we have already encountered. The more
favoured climate of the region from which the papal
audience was drawn takes us back to notions which, as
we have seen,[1] were prevalent in classical antiquity. A
further notion from a much earlier period which is em-
bedded in the speech is the antithesis between barbarism
and civilization: we cannot call the barbarians of the
northern islands Christian (we read in the chronicler's
account) *because* they live in a brutish fashion (quia more
belluino victitat). An attitude also traceable to the ancient
world—but richer for an infusion of Christian sentiment
—is the doctrine of exile and universal citizenship: this is
the Stoic 'cosmopolitanism' redressed by a doctrine of
renunciation which owes much to the teaching of St.
Augustine.[2] From a time nearer to his own day the pope

[1] Above, p. 5. On this notion of the superior martial qualities of the West,
see further below, pp. 83-4, 122.
[2] The Augustinian development is itself influenced by neo-Platonic teaching
(cf. *De Civ. Dei*, IX. 17). On this doctrine in antiquity see J. Bidez, *La cité du
monde et la cité du soleil chez les Stoiciens*, Paris 1932 (an offprint from *Bulletins
de l'Académie royale de Belgique*, Classe des lettres etc., 5th series, vol. xviii);
W. W. Tarn, *Alexander the Great*, Cambridge 1948, ii, app. 25, pp. 399-449,
esp. 401-33. I owe these references to Professor A. C. Lloyd.

is made to refer to the 'divisio apostolorum', the dispersion of the apostles over the surface of the earth.[1] But
these references to the past are, in a sense, peripheral.
What is central is the consciousness of an identity of
Christian society. Christians everywhere are brothers:
even the adherents of the scattered and doubtful communities of the East, even the members of the schismatic
Greek Church. The Christian world is one, centred on
Jerusalem, and it is the duty of all Christians to reinforce
and extend its boundaries; to 'smash the forces of the
Saracens and the devil and to spread the kingdom and
church of Christ from sea to sea'.[2] Christians at large
constitute one race, one *gens*: the world is their inheritance,
but they control only one part of it, Christendom,
Christianitas. The analogy is clear: Rome and its citizens
and its empire. In encouraging the emergence of the
concept the papacy was the only candidate for headship.

Otto of Freising, two generations earlier, had resumed
the past in just such a spirit, critical of the papacy though
he was. 'The cross', he wrote in the *Two Cities*, 'is now
worshipped by kings and has become to almost all men
the object of love and veneration.'[3] And again,

I have composed a history not of two cities but virtually of one
only, which I call the Church. For although the elect and the repro-
bate are in one household, yet I cannot call these cities two as I did
above; I must call them properly but one—composite, however, as
the grain is mixed with the chaff. . . . Since not only emperors of the
Romans but also other kings (kings of renowned realms) became
Christians, inasmuch as the sound of the word of God went out into
all the earth and unto the ends of the world, the City of Earth was laid
to rest and destined to be utterly exterminated in the end. Hence
our history is a history of the City of Christ, but that City, so long as

[1] On this see below, p. 40.
[2] A letter of 1099 quoted by P. Rousset, X Congresso Internazionale de
Scienze Storiche, Rome 1955, *Relazioni*, iii. 550. The Crusade as the *plenitudo
gentium* (cf. Isaiah xliii. 5) is most fully developed in Guibert of Nogent's
account of Urban's address: see P. Alphandéry, *La chrétienté et l'idée de Croisade*,
Paris 1954, pp. 40-1.
[3] Ed. and trans. C. C. Mierow, New York 1928, p. 283.

it is in the land of the sojourn, is 'like unto a net, that was cast into the sea', containing the good and the bad.[1]

To such concepts Innocent III lent precision and coherence. In this, as in so much else, his pontificate (1198-1216) represents a moment of clarity and definition.[2]

Gregory VII may have asserted that the Roman church was 'mistress of the whole of Christendom'.[3] Under Innocent III we even find the Greek Emperor Alexis IV (puppet of the Latins after they had attacked Constantinople) admitting the pope as 'the ecclesiastical head of the whole of Christendom'.[4] The forcible ending of the Greek schism by the victory of *Latinitas* thus for a time removed a tension within Christendom, but it was secondary in the papal view to the supreme task of advance in Asia Minor. 'I would rather that the Christians had possessed themselves of Jerusalem than Constantinople' the pope wrote in 1206[5]; and his letters contain frequent references to this *populus Christianus* which can 'possess' lands; to the 'common utility' of the Christian people; to the *terrae Christianorum*; to the *fines Christianorum*; to the *patrimonium* which is rent by civil war.[6] These notions represent the final culmination of medieval awareness of Christendom. One must, of course, be careful not to suggest that every twelfth- and thirteenth-century text labours this particular message, or is sprinkled with the word *Christianitas* in its territorial meaning. The word is not among those most frequently used by chroniclers, theologians or publicists—even by those who concern themselves with the most general political issues confronting Christian society.[7] But the consciousness of a concrete territorial

---

[1] Ed. and trans. C. C. Mierow, New York 1928, p. 324; and cf. pp. 404-5.
[2] J. Rupp, *op. cit.*, pp. 99-123.   [3] *Ibid.*, p. 55; above, p. 29.
[4] 'Totius Christianitatis caput ecclesiasticum', P.L. 215, col. 237; Rupp, 103-4.
[5] '... gratius tamen nobis fuisset si Hierusalem redacta esset in potestatem populi Christiani', P.L. 215, col. 957; Rupp, p. 110.
[6] Rupp, pp. 108-18.
[7] For example in the *Gesta Hammaburgensis* of Adam of Bremen (ed. B. Schmeidler, Script. Rer. Germ. in usum Schol., 1917), a late eleventh-century work where the expansion of Christendom is a central theme, the word

Christendom is omnipresent, an unchallenged assumption growing up over a thousand years. The terminology and habit of mind exemplified above were to strike deep roots. For centuries, as we shall see, they were to remain as established categories of speculation and of political action. Christendom and the crusade, while they slowly descended from urgent and active impulses to become the commonplaces of dull priests and scheming politicians, were not readily to be replaced by novel modes of thought.

Christianitas occurs over fifty times, but always in a transcendental sense. Over two hundred years later another work where the term might have been expected to be largely used is Pierre Dubois, *De recuperatione terrae sanctae*, ed. Langlois (1891), but the terms used are: omnes catholicos, respublica catholicorum, respublica christicolarum (pp. 3, 10, 20, 81). In Balbi's dictionary, the *Catholicon* (1286), while *christianismus* is given, *christianitas* is not: one might argue from this either the rareness of the word, or the absence of any need to explain a self-evident term.

CHAPTER 3

THE MEDIEVAL NOTION OF EUROPE
AND ITS PEOPLES

THE word Europe, which was ultimately to usurp the place of Christendom, is also, it will have been observed, used in the speech of Urban II. What was the use and significance of this term in the centuries when men thought primarily in terms of Christendom? The answer to this question is that, aside from one short episode, the name of the continent was more or less devoid of content, being found in scholarly descriptions of the *orbis* rather than in polemical writings.

Medieval geographical thought stems directly from Hellenistic and Roman antiquity as transmitted by the writers of the dark ages whom we have touched on already.[1] From Martianus Capella, Orosius, Isidore of Seville and Bede later compilers derived their picture of a tripartite world, which they described more or less fully according to their care and ambition in the use of literary sources. Direct observations or enquiry had small part in this work, and the impact of Greek scholarship through Islamic channels in the twelfth century did little to stimulate a scientific geography. 'We shall look in vain for radical changes in the content or character of the twelfth-century *liber cosmographicus*.'[2] Even in the thirteenth century there is still a general acceptance of the three continents bounded by ocean, though a more lively and independent discussion was carried on concerning questions such as the inhabited antipodes.[3] Despite the enlarged

---

[1] C. R. Beazley, *The Dawn of Modern Geography*, 3 vols., London 1897-1906, remains the fullest account in English; the best recent book is G. H. T. Kimble, *Geography in the Middle Ages*, London 1938. See above, pp. 3-7.

[2] Kimble, p. 79.   [3] *Ibid.*, pp. 83-92.

horizons of a Christendom which had learnt much of the
East during the Crusades and as a result of far-travelled
missionaries and merchants, the old stories of fantastic
peoples and weird observances, deriving ultimately from
Pliny and beyond, continued to be repeated. Long after
Marco Polo's account was available legend still dominated
the western view of the Orient[1] and an excellent summary
of current views on geography can be obtained from the
first book of the *Polichronicon* of the early fourteenth-
century writer Ranulf Higden or from the rather later
compilation which goes under the name of the *Travels* of
Sir John Mandeville. Earlier references to the superiority
of Europe to other continents are transmitted by such
writers as Higden, who records Pliny's views on the bene-
ficial effects of the European climate[2]; the Latin translation
of Aristotle's *Politics* by William Morbeke led to an awareness of a similar distinction there.[3] But such knowledge
was reminiscent or literary and lacked any actuality.

The encyclopaedists from Isidore and Bede down to
Vincent of Beauvais, Albertus Magnus and Brunetto
Latini thus give a conventional description of Europe,
Africa and Asia. So do writers who comment on the Old
Testament and it is worth while considering this in rather
more detail, for here we shall find that an element which
might have contributed to the continents acquiring emotional associations,[4] in fact had little influence in that
direction.

The association of Shem with Asia, Ham with Africa
and Japheth with Europe finds its place in all commentaries on Genesis. Typical of these is the catechetical
work of Alcuin[5]:

---

[1] Cf. L. Olschki, *Storia letteraria delle scoperte geografiche*, Florence 1937; and
R. Wittkower, 'Marvels of the East: A study in the history of Monsters',
Journal of the Warburg and Courtauld Institutes, v (1942), 159-97 and esp. 182-93.
[2] *Polichronicon*, R.S., i. 50-52.
[3] Cf. above, p. 5, and R. Koebner, 'Despot and despotism: Vicissitudes of
a political term', *Journal of the Warburg and Courtauld Institutes*, xiv (1951),
279-82.   [4] See above, p. 8.
[5] *Interrogationes et responsiones in Genesim*, P.L. 100, col. 532: '*Inter.* 141:

Q. How was the world divided by the sons and grandsons of Noah? *A.* Shem is regarded as acquiring Asia, Ham Africa, and Japheth Europe.

Q. How many different races did they beget? *A.* To Japheth were born 15 sons, to Ham 30 and to Shem 27. This makes a total of 72 from which 72 races arose, among whom the Lord sent 72 disciples.

Q. Why do we read: God shall enlarge Japheth and he shall dwell in the tents of Shem? *A.* The Hebrews originated with Shem, the Gentiles with Japheth. The multitude of the faithful has been spread abroad—and Japheth's name meaning enlargement portends this. As for 'shall dwell in the tents of Shem', this was prophesied of us since, following on the rejection of the people of Israel, we enjoy the knowledge of the wisdom of the scriptures.

These observations are for the most part taken practically word for word from St. Jerome[1] and were to be repeated by other writers. Some of these are more careful than others: Hugh of St. Victor painstakingly points out that Japheth's sons had the north of Asia as well as Europe.[2] Others have their small addition to make to the interpretative tradition, like the ninth-century writer who explains that the enlargement of Japheth means not only the Christian inheritance of inspired knowledge, but 'in historical terms was fulfilled by the Roman occupation of Judaea'[3]; and the tenth-century writer who takes up again St. Augustine's suggestion[4] that the descendants of Ham are heretics.[5]

But a more significant feature of later comment is its

Quomodo divisus est orbis a filiis et nepotibus Noe? *Resp.* Sem, ut aestimatur, Asiam, Cham Africam, et Japhet Europam sortitus est. *Inter.* 142: Quot gentes singuli eorum procrearunt? *Resp.* De Japhet nati sunt filii quindecim, de Cham triginta, de Sem viginti septem: simul septuaginta duo, de quibus ortae sunt gentes septuaginta duae, inter quas misit Dominus discipulos septuaginta duos. *Inter.* 143: Cur dictum est: 'Dilatet Deus Japhet etc.'? *Resp.* De Sem Hebraei, de Japhet populus gentium nascitur. Quia igitur lata est multitudo credentium, a latitudine, quae Japhet dicitur, latitudo nomen accepit. Quod additur 'Habitet in tabernaculis Sem', de nobis prophetatur qui in eruditione scientiae Scripturarum, ejecto Israele, versamur.'

[1] Above, p. 12.

[2] 'Filii Japhet obtinuerunt septentrionalem partem Asiae et totam Europam.' *Adnotationes . . . in pentateuchon,* P.L. 175, col. 49.

[3] Angelôme of Luxeuil, *Comment. in Genesim,* P.L. 115, col. 163: 'Sed tunc completum est historialiter quando Romani Judaeam ceperunt.'

[4] Above, p. 12.

[5] Rémy of St. Germain d'Auxerre, *Comment. in Genesim,* P.L. 131, col. 80.

insistence on the oecumenical character of the Christian church. The most obvious occasion for such a development was reflection on the mission of the apostles to the world at large. This was to lead to the view that the *orbis* had been parcelled out to the immediate followers of Christ: the world was the field in the parables of the sower and the mustard seed (Matthew xiii. 3-8, 18-32):

> The east was given to Thomas and Bartholomew, the south to Simon and Matthew, the north to Philip and Thadeus, the middle of the world to Matthias and James, the Mediterranean provinces to John and Andrew, and the kingdoms of the west to Peter and Paul.[1]

We have noticed[2] that this 'divisio apostolorum' was re-called by Pope Urban in Malmesbury's account of the speech at Clermont. It was a widely influential picture of the church in relation with political geography, and is found fully worked out in, for example, the pages of Otto of Freising.[3] But from the viewpoint of the continents more might have been expected of comment on the key text in Matthew xiii. 33:

> 'The Kingdom of Heaven is like unto leaven, which a woman took and hid in three measures of meal, till the whole was leavened.'

Raban Maur and Paschasius Radbert, both writing in the mid-ninth century, take the parable as meaning the dispersion of the church through the progeny of the three sons of Noah[4] and in the twelfth century Anselm of Laon applies the three measures of meal to the three continents[5]:

> The three measures signify the three virtues . . . or the three kinds of men . . . or all the faithful gathered together from the three parts of the world, Asia, Africa and Europe, or from the three sons of Noah.

---

[1] Quoted from M. Paris, *Historia Major*, R.S., i. 101, who depends here on Raban Maur, *De vita Beati Mariae Magdalenae*, P.L. 112, col. 1491. The names and areas of the apostles vary in various lists.

[2] Above, p. 34. The *Festum divisionis apostolorum* fell on 15 July.

[3] *The Two Cities*, ed. Mierow, pp. 238-9. Peter the Venerable uses the word 'Europa' in a reference to the *divisio Apostolorum*, P.L. 189, col. 695.

[4] Raban Maur, *De Universo*, xii, cap. ii, P.L. 111, Col. 333; Paschasius Radbert, *Expositio in Matthaeum*, P.L. 120, col. 499.

[5] 'Tria Sata, tres sunt virtutes . . . vel tria genera hominum significant. Vel omnes fideles ex tribus partibus mundi collectos, Asia, Africa et Europa, vel ex tribus filiis Noe natos.' *Enarrationes in Matthaeum*, P.L. 162, col. 1375.

This line of thought could scarcely fail to affect the meaning attached to the Genesis story. In another twelfth century commentator we find such a development. Robert of Tuy concludes his summary[1] of the meaning of the dispersion of Noah's sons by saying that thereby

the three parts of the world were filled by the descendants of the three, in which the Church of Christ, demonstrating the faith of the Holy Trinity, was prefigured.

The twelfth century, as we have seen, was the age when an expanding Christendom was much in men's minds.

It might have been anticipated that the theologians were scarcely likely to endow the continents with different characteristics derived from the three sons of Noah. The moralists were only a little more imaginative. In an Anglo-Saxon miscellany containing information about Biblical characters we find the writer making an inference not entirely surprising:

And undoubtedly from these three men, Noah's sons, all this world was afterwards born, though the Lord divided them in three strains and genealogies; and he made a division according to the blame with which they blamed their father Noah, in that he separated those genealogies in three: namely in servile and churlish race and noble race.[2]

Such a classification was capable of making for a superiority in one of the continents as against the others. This conclusion is nearly reached in the fourteenth-century Northumbrian poem, the *Cursor Mundi*. Here we find, immediately after the allocation of the continents to the three sons of Noah, a plainer statement:

> Knyth, and thrall, and freman,
> Oute of per thre breper bigan;
> O sem freman, o Iaphet knytht,
> thrall of cham pe maledight.[3]

[1] *De trinitate et operibus ejus*, P.L. 167, col. 364: ' . . . ut tres partes mundi a trium generatione implerentur, in quibus etiam Ecclesia Christi sanctae Trinitatis fide explananda praemonstrabatur'.

[2] Tiberius A.3, f. 43, printed by Napier, *Anglia*, xi (1888–9), 2–3. I owe the reference and the translation to Professor D. Whitelock.

[3] E.E.T.S., i. 130.

This is a translation into social, or class, terminology of the Augustinian distinction between the damned progeny of Ham, those who are called, and those who are justified.[1] The poem, however, while it gets near to a continental antithesis derived from this approach, does not really take the final step. The tradition of social origin stemming from the three sons of Noah did not entirely die out[2] but it was not elaborated as it might have been. Despite St. Augustine's hints, the church universal transcended the divisions of the *orbis*, however predetermined or natural these might be considered to be. But what of the historians, whose universal chronicles so often involved a consideration of the description of early history given in Genesis? Here, too, we find a general repetition of the facts, and virtually no inferences drawn from them.

The English chroniclers may be cited as convenient examples. The fully developed St. Albans' *Chronicle* of Matthew Paris records the division of the earth among the sons of Noah,[3] just as it records—as a 'gentile fable' —the rape of Europa[4] and the 'divisio apostolorum'.[5] And so with practically all of the chronicles which start their narratives from the creation of the world—such as the Malmesbury compilation known as the *Eulogium historiarum*,[6] Higden's *Polichronicon*,[7] as well as other St. Albans' works such as Wendover before Paris's time and the *Flores historiarum* afterwards. There are points of interest in these traditional accounts. Higden, for example, records Isidore of Seville's rationalizing of the Europa myth[8] and he and others often refer to a fourth son of Noah, Ionithus (or Ionicus) by name. This last invention seems to have been produced in the Byzantine

---

[1] Above, p. 12.   [2] Below, p. 107.
[3] *Historia Major*, ed. Luard, R.S., i. 5 (from the *Historia Scholastica* of Petrus Comestor).
[4] *Ibid.*, i. 13 (from Augustine).   [5] Above, p. 40, n. 1.
[6] R.S., ed. F. S. Haydon, i. 28-9, etc.
[7] R.S., ed. C. Babbington, ii. 246-8, etc.   [8] ii. 340-2.

Empire in the late seventh century by the author of the *Revelationes divinae* which circulated under the name of St. Methodius. This pseudo-Methodius, short and exhilaratingly apocalyptic, was already available in Latin versions by the eighth century; it maintained its popularity in the West until the sixteenth century.[1] Its frequent occurrence in historical works was clearly due to its incorporation in the extremely influential *Historia Scholastica* of the twelfth-century writer, Petrus Comestor.[2] But beyond repeating the assertion of Petrus Comestor and his source the chroniclers[3] do no more to develop the potentialities of the fourth son.

There was, however, one aspect of the Genesis story that received a good deal of elaboration. The Teutonic tribes were possessors of a profound interest in their ancestors: the Bible indicated that all men were descended from Noah and his sons; it was an obvious step to close the gap by creating pedigrees which linked together the personages descended from Noah and the legendary founders of the peoples of Europe. To this task the chroniclers of every country in Christendom addressed themselves and the results may still be read in the early chapters—usually neglected by historians for the very good reason that they are non-historical—of nearly all the great national narratives. Here again for convenience we must restrict ourselves to the example offered by British writers.

One must stress the word 'British', for the earliest of such inventions occurs in the ninth-century *Historia Brittonum* associated with the name of Nennius.[4] The text is

---

[1] It is reprinted in several of the older patristic collections. I consulted the text given by M. de la Bigne, *Magna Bibliotheca Veterum Patrum*, Cologne 1618-22, iii. 363-70. For the influence of the pseudo-Methodius see A. R. Anderson, *Alexander's Gate, Gog and Magog, and the Enclosed Nations*, Medieval Academy of America, Cambridge, Mass., 1932, esp. pp. 44-9.

[2] Ed. Paris (J. Frellon) 1513, fo. xv.   [3] E.g. *Eulogium* i. 29; Higden ii. 246-8

[4] Here used in the edition of T. Mommsen, M.G.H., Auct. Ant., Chron. Min. iii. F. Liebermann strongly argues that the whole work is by Nennius (with later interpolations), *Essays in Medieval History presented to T. F. Tout*, Manchester 1925, pp. 30-33.

as obscure as it is early. It is sufficient here to note that scattered throughout the *Historia Brittonum* are genealogies of the British race and of the German peoples who invaded the British Isles in the fifth and sixth centuries. There are two quite contrary accounts of the origin of the British. One of these represents Brutus, the eponymous founder of the Britains, as descended from Ham; the other as descended from Japheth. The generations are traced back in the first case to Silvius (Brutus's father), who was the son of Aeneas and descended from Jupiter and Saturn, themselves deriving from Zoroaster the grandson of Ham. This tradition Mommsen considered to have been influenced by early glosses on the *Georgics* of Virgil and from Jerome.[1] Even more probably it is a later embellishment due to an interpolator who was familiar with the Troy legend.[2] The second genealogy is much fuller and may be set out as in diagram opposite.[3] Only parts of this table are susceptible of clear explanation.[4] From Japheth to Elisa derives from Genesis (Iavan, Elisa). The compiler himself was aware that little scriptural authority attaches to the list he gives beyond this point for he goes on[5]:

> But Japheth had seven sons. From the first, named Gomer, descended the Galli; from the second, Magog, the Scythi and Gothi; from the third, Madain, the Medes; from the fourth, Iuvan, the Greeks; from the fifth, Tubal, arose the Hiberei, Hispani and Itali; from the sixth, Mosoch, sprang the Cappadoceans, and from the seventh, named Tiras, descended the Thracians.

Here the author is repeating the etymological ingenuities of Josephus and Jerome. The material lying between

[1] The tables are in the cited edition pp. 149-52; see Mommsen's notes pp. 150-3.

[2] This is particularly likely in view of the repetition of much of the material quoted (§ 10) as an appendage (§ 18) to the genealogy of Alanus (§ 17).

[3] *Ibid.*, pp. 159-62. In § 7 (p. 147) there is another reference to 'Isiocon', son of Alanus, and father of 'Britto'.

[4] See Mommsen's notes on pp. 159, 161-2.

[5] This is § 18 of the *Historia Brittonum*. For a reference to Jerome's commentary see above, p. 39.

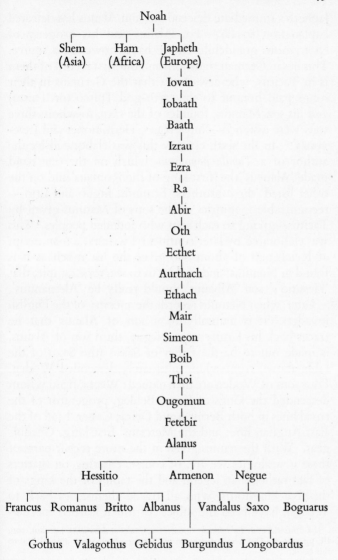

Noah

Shem (Asia)   Ham (Africa)   Japheth (Europe)

Iovan

Iobaath

Baath

Izrau

Ezra

Ra

Abir

Oth

Ecthet

Aurthach

Ethach

Mair

Simeon

Boib

Thoi

Ougomun

Fetebir

Alanus

Hessitio   Armenon   Negue

Francus Romanus Britto Albanus   Vandalus Saxo Boguarus

Gothus Valagothus Gebidus Burgundus Longobardus

Japheth's immediate descendants and Alanus has defeated explanation so far.[1] For Alanus and his progeny of eponymous grandchildren we have, however, a source. This lies in German traditions and our first record of them is in Tacitus, where we learn that the Germans in their songs paid honour to the earth-god Tuisco (or Tuisto) and his son Mannus, founder of the race, to whom three sons were assigned—'Ingaevones, Herminones and Istaevones'.[2] In the sixth century this was elaborated by the author of a *Tabula populorum* which on the one hand made 'Alaneus' the 'first king of the Romans' and on the other listed 'three brothers, Erminus, Inguo and Istio'— recognizable memories of the sons of Mannus given by Tacitus—giving to each sons who founded peoples.[3] This was elaborated by later continental writers: a manuscript at Reichenau of about 800 gives the list much as it is found in Nennius[4] and enables us to see, for example, that 'Hessitio's' son 'Albanus' should really be 'Alemannus'.

Later, when Nennius records the ancestry of the English invaders,[5] it is naturally to a son of Alanus that he traces back his family tree. Negue, third son of Alanus, is made out to be the father of Saxus (the Saxo of the table above) from whom ultimately descended Woden. Four sons of Woden are then named: Wecta, from whom descended the kings of Kent; Beldeg, progenitor of the royal lines in both Bernicia and Deira; Casser, head of the East Anglian line; and the Mercians' first king, Guedolgeat. With the names given in the more recent parts of these genealogies we are, of course, entering on matters of fact rather than legend and the tables of the kings of the five kingdoms, who all traced themselves back to Woden, have been the subject of much learned specula-

---

[1] Edmund Faral, *La Légende Arthurienne: études et documents*, i (1929), app. III, pp. 295-7. The whole discussion of Nennius above owes a good deal to this book.

[2] I paraphrase the passage in the *Germania*, 2: note that Tacitus gives names of tribes, not persons.

[3] Faral, *op. cit.*, pp. 83-4, and refs.   [4] Ed. Mommsen, p. 159 n. 4.

[5] §§ 31, 58-61; ed. Mommsen pp. 171, 202-5.

tion for the light they shed on the early history of the English.[1] But between Woden and Negue we are again in the mists of legend and the mystery is particularly dense which surrounds Negue's great grandson, Geat, who (says the *Historia Brittonum* cryptically) was 'the son of a god, but not the Omnipotent'.[2]

Geat and Woden also figure in the *Anglo-Saxon Chronicle* as the ancestors of Ida (s.a. 547) and of Aethelwulf (s.a. 853).[3] The chief interest of the *Chronicle*, however, as of Aethelwerd and Asser's *Life of Alfred*, is that they take the predecessors of Alfred back to an individual 'who was born in the ark'. In the Parker text of the *Chronicle* this is stated to be Hrathra; in the B and C texts, as in Aethelwerd,[4] the name given is Scef or Sceaf; and in Asser we read as the last entry 'Seth qui fuit Noe'.[5] The interest for us in these transactions is that they were to provide Alfred with a Semitic origin. There can, one supposes, be no doubt that H. M. Chadwick was correct in suggesting that an ancient folk memory of a boy who came in a boat to Scania lies behind the Scef of Aethelwerd and the *Chronicle*. Thus the Hrathra or Scef 'who was born in the ark' really meant originally 'who was born in a boat', and has nothing to do with Noah at all.[6] But Asser's reading of Scef was Seth and later writers, hunting in vain for a son of Noah who corresponded to this name, made the obvious emendation to Shem (Sem in the

---

[1] For a survey of recent work on this subject and a fresh assessment see K. Sisam, 'Anglo-Saxon Royal Genealogies', *Proceedings of the British Academy*, xxxix (1953), 287-348.

[2] It has been suggested that Geat recalls the Gapt referred to in Jornandes, *De rebus Geticis*, cap. 14; though there are difficulties in this (Chadwick, *Origin of the English Nation*, Cambridge 1924, p. 253). Jornandes is a mid-sixth-century historian of the Goths.

[3] Ed. G. N. Garmonsway, 'Everyman Library', 1953, pp. 16, 66; and see K. Sisam, *op. cit.*, *passim*.

[4] Garmonsway, p. 66 n. 4.

[5] Ed. W. H. Stevenson, Oxford 1904, p. 3.

[6] Chadwick, *op. cit.*, pp. 257-8 and see the whole of chapter xi. The argument largely turns on the Scyld Scefing of *Beowulf*. Malmesbury, R.S., i. 121, has a fuller account of the legend than Aethelwerd, but in Malmesbury Scef appears twice in the list, being given in the first case as 'Strephius ... fuit filius Noae in arca natus'. On this see Sisam, *op. cit.* pp. 314-20.

Vulgate text). So it is that in Matthew Paris (to omit the intervening chroniclers on whom he depended) we find Alfred's lineage ascending to Noah by way of Shem[1]— this despite the adherence of Paris to the allocation of Europe to Japheth which we have noticed,[2] and to the existence at St. Albans of the tradition of the line from Japheth down to Alanus.[3]

We have thus seen the British traditions which trace national origins to Japheth or to Ham and the English traditions which trace them to Scef or Seth or Shem. All these stories, though often transmitted by later compilers, were swept away by the general acceptance from the twelfth century onwards of the Trojan origins of the British and of other continental peoples.

The Trojan origin of the Franks is a learned fiction first found in the Frankish chronicle known by the name of its supposed author, Fredegarius.[4] The compiler, or compilers, of this were at work in the seventh century and proceeded partly by summarizing the chronicle of Jerome, Isidore of Seville and Gregory of Tours, partly by giving a vivid imagination full scope.[5] In the result a Duke Francio emerged as the first leader of one section of the expatriate Trojans, while in volunteering a King Torquatus as leader of the other half of the exiles, 'Fredegarius' was to start a myth of the Trojan origin of the Turks which had an almost equally long life. Francio or Francus was soon widely accepted among Franks and non-Franks. The Trojan origin is repeated in the *Liber historiae*

---

[1] *Historia Major*, R.S., i. 403; Cf. Hoveden, i. 35, Wendover, i. 9-10, Richard of Cirencester, i. 242-3, ii. 4-5 (R.S.).   [2] Above, p. 42.

[3] See the 'distinctio regionum' in the *Flores Historiarum*, R.S., i. 5-6 where the Nennius table is more or less reproduced (above, p. 45), though Negue is credited with four sons (Wandalus, Saxon, Bogarus, Targus) much as in the early MS. quoted by Mommsen in his edition p. 159 n. 4.

[4] M.G.H., Script. Rer. Mer. ii (ed. B. Krusch), pp. 45-6, 199-200.

[5] For a full discussion see Faral, *op. cit.*, pp. 171-83, and appendix i (pp. 262-93), G. Kurth, *Histoire poétique des Mérovingiens*, Brussells-Leipzig 1893, pp. 85-99, 505-16; Professor J. M. Wallace-Hadrill kindly allowed me to consult him on these questions.

Francorum (c. 727), a work more popular even than 'Fredegarius'; it is found (as we have seen) in the *Historia Brittonum*; by the first quarter of the twelfth century the legend was incorporated in a dozen different texts.[1] Some other peoples found authors who performed for them the grafting operation which attached their progenitors to the noble stock of Troy. Dudo of Saint-Quentin provided the Normans with such a descent in the tenth century.[2] And, most influential of all, Geoffrey of Monmouth in his *Historia Regum* (1147) vulgarized the legend in respect of Brutus and Britain, establishing a tradition which (despite a handful of sceptics) was to go virtually unchallenged until the sixteenth and seventeenth centuries,[3] and which was almost as widely read (in French adaptations) on the continent as in these islands. The Trojan origin was hooked on to the descent from Japheth *via* Alanus and further speculation on post-diluvian ancestry was mainly elaboration of the Troy theme.[4] The diffusion of interest was accelerated by the *Roman de Troie*, written in the twelfth century by Benoît de Sainte-Maure. From one end of Europe to the other the early chapters of historical works were coloured by Trojan origins.[5] As Henry of Huntingdon observed in the mid-twelfth century and Higden repeated in the mid-fourteenth, most nations derived their origins from Troy.[6]

The foregoing pages have summarized attempts by the writers of history in the dark and early middle ages to combine memories of folk origins with the inspired account in Genesis, with what help they could find in the sources of Latin antiquity and the Fathers of the church.

[1] E.g. Widukind, P.L. 137, col. 124; Aimoin, P.L. 139, cols. 637-40; and cf. Faral, pp. 288-9. [2] Faral, pp. 288-93.

[3] Sir Thomas Kendrick, *British Antiquity*, London 1950, touches on many aspects of this. [4] E.g. *Eulogium Historiarum*, i. 301-2.

[5] See A. Joly, *Benoît de Sainte-More et le roman de Troie*, Paris 1870, pp. 123-40 for twelfth- and thirteenth-century evidence from different parts of the continent.

[6] Huntingdon: 'Sicut pleraeque gentes Europae, ita Franci a Trojanis duxerunt originem', R.S., p. 248; Higden: 'Gens etiam Francorum, sicut pleraeque gentes Europae, a Trojanis originem duxit', R.S., i. 272.

Some of these developments were to have a very significant influence in literature—as with the story of Troy, of
Brutus and of Arthur. But it would be wrong to suggest
that these matters bulk large in the medieval chronicle.
They do not. More often they are included as perfunctory
tributes to a saga tradition and to the genealogical preoccupations of the historical books in the Old Testament.
Above all they show very little concern with the peopling
of Europe and display no attempt to associate the continent as such with the Christian faith. After all, we have
seen that, as early as 'Fredegarius', the notion was expounded that the Turks, too, were descended from the
refugees from Troy. Admittedly for 'Fredegarius' the
'Torci', if they meant anything, meant a remote and unimportant tribe in the heart of Asia. But by the end of the
eleventh century the Turks were closer at hand, established in Egypt, parts of Asia Minor and, above all, in
Jerusalem whence they were driven by the First Crusade.
From then onwards *Teucri* or *Turci* bulk large in the
annals of the Crusade and as early as the *Historia Hierosoly-
mitana* of Baudri de Bourgueil (c. 1107) the relationship
between Turks and Franks, both descended from Trojans
(and both, it may be added, hostile still to the Greeks),
was stressed.[1] Francus and Turcus were remembered in
the Saint-Denis scriptorium and in due course figured in
the *Grandes Chroniques de France*.[2] This fraternizing between Franks and Turks, theoretical though it may have
been, could scarcely have developed had the genealogies
we have been discussing been regarded as involving
genuine cultural or political consequences.[3]

The crusades, one might have thought, might well
have stimulated a revival of the Greek notion that there
was a natural hostility between East and West, between
Asia and Europe. The attitude of the crusaders certainly
encouraged the Greeks to regard them as barbarians, but

[1] Joly, p. 526n.
[2] Joly, 525-6; *Grandes Chroniques* i. 6-7, 9.   [3] Cf. below, pp. 84-5, 109.

a continental antithesis as such was not readily developed in Byzantium, which straddled Asia and Europe.[1] In the West the polarity was occasionally noticed but not regarded as important. Otto of Freising saw the East as less perfect than the West, but did not elaborate the idea.[2] Another twelfth-century source writes: 'the West rose against the East, Europe against Asia'.[3] Yet these are fugitive apprehensions and could scarcely flourish in an atmosphere where the global mission of Christianity was still regarded as the prime issue.

Throughout the centuries up to and including the thirteenth the word Europe itself is thus rarely met with in passages other than those descriptive of geographical situation. Yet there was one occasion when the word was used with something more than purely conventional meaning. That it was in the event not to have much effect is one of the interesting features of the episode. Charles the Great is described by some of his contemporaries as the 'father of Europe', 'the worshipful head of Europe' and so on.[4] There is an element of literary artificiality in this; but it undoubtedly expresses something deeper and more real than mere poetical or rhetorical elaboration. It depends in fact on the contemporary identification of Christianity with *Romanitas*: the *Romani* were those Christians who were not *Graeci*; and of these 'Romans' the head was Charlemagne, whose rule over Europe corresponded with the rule over Eastern Christians exercised by the emperor at Constantinople.[5] (This,

[1] Cf. the use of Asia and Europe in, e.g., the *Alexiad* of Anna Comnena, ed. Leib, 3 vols., Paris 1937-45, iii, index *s.nn.*

[2] *Two Cities*, ed. Mierow, pp. 322-3.

[3] C. Kohler, 'Un sermon commémoratif de la prise de Jérusalem par les croisés, attribué à Foucher de Chartres', *Revue de l'Orient Latin*, viii (1900-1), 162.

[4] 'Rex pater Europae', 'Rex Karolus . . . Europae venerandus apex', quoted by W. Ullmann, *The Growth of Papal Government in the Middle Ages*, London 1955, p. 95; notes 3 and 4 give references to discussions of the term Europa, to which should be added Heinz Gollwitzer, 'Zur Wortgeschichte und Sinndeutung von "Europa"', *Saeculum*, ii (Munich 1951), 161-71.

[5] Ullmann, pp. 61-4, 88, 89.

of course, denied the unity of the Christian world, of which the Byzantine emperors conceived themselves to be the undisputed masters.[1]) Charlemagne's role

was none other than that of the true monarch in the West, of the monarch ruling over that entity which was called *Europa* by some, and the *imperium Christianum* by others, and also *imperium Romanum* by still others: . . . the empire under Charlemagne's rule was that entity which was held together by the Christian faith as expounded by the Roman church.[2]

The imperial connection with this 'Roman' Europe was not entirely forgotten by later ages. Widukind of Corvey calls Henry I the 'greatest king in Europe'; the bounds of the empire can be described as covering 'almost the whole of Europe'; the 'Italians, the French and the Germans are the three outstanding races of Europe'.[3] But it was, of course, the papacy which was to inherit the Carolingian theocracy and it was the papacy which gradually evolved those concepts of the 'populus dei', the 'societas fidelium', the 'res publica Christiana' which were to be caught up in the larger notion of Christendom, as already described.[4] For Gregory VII the Roman empire was certainly Christian: 'Christ rules where Augustus ruled'. But this Christian society was larger than that: 'The law of the popes embraces more territory than does imperial law.'[5] Europe is thus by the eleventh century largely *démodé*, an outworn concept, a memory only of the ninth-century situation where the reality was two territorial empires and not one potentially universal church.[6]

[1] G. Ostrogorsky, *History of the Byzantine State*, Oxford 1956, p. 165.

[2] Ullmann, p. 105.

[3] Gollwitzer, *op. cit.*, citing M.G.H., *Scriptores*, iii. 435; xv (1). 359; Ullmann, pp. 236-7; and cf. *Carmina Cantabrigiensia*, ed. W. Bulst, Heidelberg 1950, p. 40.

[4] Above, pp. 29, 35; Ullmann, pp. 167-95, 271-6.

[5] 'Quibus imperavit Augustus, imperavit Christus'; 'Plus enim Terrarum lex Romanorum pontificum quam imperatorum obtinuit' (*Register*, ii. 237); cited Ullmann, p. 276.

[6] Cf. the three occasions for its use in Adam of Bremen (above, p. 35 n. 7): one is geographical (I. iii), one a recollection of the Carolingian attitude (I. xiv) and only one has a more general bearing: 'Civitas Iumne . . .Est sane maxima omnium, quas Europa claudit, civitatum' (II. xxii).

The attitudes of mind adopted in the literary sources we have been discussing are also in certain ways reflected in the graphic art of the period and in the depiction of the universe in maps. The possibility of Noah's three sons symbolizing the continents did not apparently appeal to the illuminator or the sculptor. While Noah bulks large in the iconography of the middle ages, Japheth, Shem and Ham figure only in the drunkenness scene.[1] As for Europa, we have seen that in classical antiquity there was a substantial artistic tradition of the story of the rape,[2] and this seems to have continued unbroken for a time in the Greek atmosphere of Byzantium.[3] But in the Latin West the myth produced few and unimportant memorials. The pictured Europa lacks life even as a mythological figure and acquired none as typifying the western world.[4]

The geographers were, it would seem, no more anxious to appropriate Europa than the artists.[5] The *mappaemundi* exist in scores of manuscripts and much work needs to be done before secure generalizations may be based upon them.[6] Nonetheless they afford an artless and unself-conscious view of the world as contemporaries saw it and one which tallies in most respects with that derived from other sources.

The majority of medieval world maps were literary in

[1] D. C. Allen, *The Legend of Noah* (Illinois Studies in Language and Literature, xxxiii), Urbana 1949, pp. 155-63, with copious references.

[2] Above, p. 5.

[3] K. Weizmann, *Greek Mythology in Byzantine Art*, Princeton 1951, pp. 183-6.

[4] See, e.g., the index s.v. 'Europa' in F. Saxl und H. Meier, *Verzeichnis astrologischer und mythologischer illustrierter Handschriften des Lateinischen Mittelalters*, 2 vols., London 1953; and cf. the Lyons MS. illustrated in E. Panofsky, *Studies in Iconology*, New York 1939, plate VII. See further below, p. 103.

[5] See references to Beazley and Kimble, above, p. 37; and the rapid survey with excellent references in Dana B. Durand, *The Vienna-Klosterneuburg Map Corpus*, Leiden 1952, pp. 3-29.

[6] Our knowledge of *mappaemundi* owes much to the labours of the late Michael C. Andrews, whose collection of about 500 drawings and photographs is now deposited with the Royal Geographical Society. I have to thank this Society and especially Mr. G. R. Crone for providing me with facilities for consulting the Andrews' collection. Andrews himself made a tentative analysis of the material in 'Study and classification of medieval mappae mundi', *Archaeologia*, lxxv (London 1926), 61-74.

origin and intention. They made no pretence of repre-
senting an accurate picture of the countries of the world
seen together—even if occasionally a map of a more
accurate kind is found of a small area. The elements of
ancient geography were digested to a form which is often
little more than a diagrammatic representation of the
three continents in symmetrical arrangement (the T-O
maps so-called) or equally stark representations of the two
hemispheres, showing zones or climates. Elaboration of
these basic patterns could on occasion be carried to great
lengths, as in the great wall-map at Hereford, though
maps by themselves are rarities before the end of the
thirteenth century. They normally occur only as illustrations of a favourite text—Isidore of Seville, Sallust,
William of Conches, and Macrobius' commentary on the
Somnium Scipionis.

From the view-point of this study we must note that
a considerable number of maps illustrated the diffusion
of Noah's sons, particularly in amplification of Isidore of
Seville, and that the *divisio apostolorum* was also expressed
cartographically. But the Isidore maps show only the
simplest form of association between the continents and
Japheth, Shem and Ham: see plate I (*b*). There is no elaboration here of the notion that the descendants of Japheth
were to be the Christian races.[1] Similarly the 'Beatus'
maps showing the evangelizing of the earth do not indicate that the most permanent conversion was effected in
Europe.[2] As for the names of the continents, they had
probably little enough significance; how else can one
explain, in so elaborate an example as the wall-map at
Hereford, the transposal of 'Europa' and 'Affrica', an
'error' which could scarcely have occurred if the words

[1] In some Isidore manuscripts the names of the three sons of Noah entirely
replace the names of the continents. These form the category termed by
Andrews '□ and V': the box contains the V and in the three sections occur
the names of Japheth, Shem and Ham. There are 27 such examples in the
Andrews' collection.
[2] For the 'Beatus' maps see Beazley ii. 549-559 and illustrations.

had meant anything.[1] It may at first appear strange that there was apparently not a single attempt made to indicate Christendom as such on medieval maps; that the word *Christianitas* does not appear in *mappaemundi*; that the frontiers of Christian territory are nowhere indicated.[2] But, as we have seen, so long as the notion was a living notion, Christendom was potentially the whole earth. The full development of this sentiment we have traced to the twelfth century; by the time a more realistic cartography emerges at the end of the thirteenth century, Christendom was beginning to pass away.

[1] *The World Map of Richard of Haldingham*, with a memoir by G. R. Crone, The Royal Geographical Society, 1954, memoir p. 4.

[2] I venture on this generalization on the basis of an examination of the Andrews' collection. For two dubious and late exceptions, see below, p. 95. Even so ingenious a cartographic symbolist as Opicinus de Canistris does not distinguish Christendom as such; see ref. below, p. 93, n. 1.

CHAPTER 4

THE DISINTEGRATION OF CHRISTENDOM

I N the preceding chapter we have seen that Christendom was the largest unit to which men in the Latin west felt allegiance in the middle ages. The word 'Christianitas' had a number of synonyms: 'respublica Christiana', 'populus Christianus' and other similar expressions are frequently met with in the serious literature of the central middle ages. It was, of course, essentially an idea which meant more to the classes who determined politics, religious and secular, in the period, to the higher clergy, the baronage and the great merchants, than it did to humbler persons whose horizons were circumscribed by the narrower limits of hamlet or township. Yet the very existence of a vernacular noun 'Christian', meaning no more (and no less) than 'person' gives a vivid indication that religion rather than race or government or geography formed the common basis of all groups in western society. To be a Christian meant full humanity in opposition to the brute beasts.

Above all, this is the terminology of the Crusades, when the Latin West forcibly took cognizance of the outside world. In the last resort, as has been noted above, Christendom embraced all Christians and included the schismatic or irregular Christian communities of the East. All through the period of genuine crusading from the eleventh century to the thirteenth, 'Christians' is the word we find in the sources to describe all those who took an active part in the crusading effort and even in the fourth crusade, when the Latin Christians battened on the Greek Christians, we still find the word used in western sources to cover the Greeks as well as the Romans.[1] More significantly the word 'nostri', our men, is commonly found describing the Christian soldiers fighting in Asia Minor. In this acceptance of an active and aggressive Christendom uncommitted to any single continent, there are hints that the very difficulties and dangers of the enterprise produced a sense of estrangement between western Christians and their outposts in Syria and Palestine. For these lands were 'ultra mare', beyond the sea, 'la terre que crestiens tenoient par delà la mer', 'la sainte terre d'oultremer'. No member of a twentieth-century European country with colonial dependencies can fail to see that in inventing an 'Overseas', an 'Outremer', the West was admitting—subconsciously and hesitantly maybe—a division in the unity of Christendom.

That this was of secondary importance in the middle ages is, however, evident from the scarcity of examples of the word Europe in our sources. The copious use of the word which may have been suggested by earlier pages of this book is illusory, for practically all the examples come from those passages of exegesis or description where the word is scarcely avoidable: they come from the early pages of the chronicles where the dispersion of mankind is in question, not from later passages dealing with the political events of the twelfth, thirteenth or fourteenth centuries. Ernest Langlois found only four instances of 'Europe' to record in his index of the proper names in the Chansons de Geste.[2] In the *Great Chronicle* of Matthew Paris, composed at St. Albans in the mid-thirteenth century, there is, I think, only one occasion when the word Europe is used in the very full and detailed narrative of European politics written by Paris himself, and cover-

---

[1] E.g. Robert de Clari, *La Conquête de Constantinople*, ed. P. Lauer, C.F.M.A., carefully distinguishes between 'Grice' on the one hand and Venetians and 'li pelerins, li croisié' on the other, but writes (p. 16) of a Greek emperor as 'li plus rikes de tous les crestiens'.

[2] *Tables des noms propres . . . dans les Chansons de Geste imprimées*, Paris 1904: since this date doubtless a few other examples must have occurred.

ing the years 1232 to 1259,[1] though it is common enough in St. Albans accounts of the earliest times.[2] If we look at another compilation of not dissimilar character, the *Grandes Chroniques de France*, which in their vernacular form were put together at Saint-Denis in the late fourteenth century, we find a similar state of affairs. The word Europe is used three times: once to describe the legendary migrations of the Franks, once to describe the conquests of the Saracens, once to indicate the boundary between the continents at the Bosphorus[3]—and on each occasion the word is devoid of any meaning beyond the strictly geographical. On the other hand the Chronicle of Saint-Denis uses the word Christendom not only more often but also more richly: Christendom has a head (the pope), a knighthood, a profit and a loss, a government and a history.[4] If one wants to compare like with like one can say either that the king of France and the emperor are 'the most powerful rulers in Christendom',[5] or that the king of France is the most splendid among all Christian princes.[6] Europe, one must conclude, is a word devoid of sentiment, Christendom a word with profound emotional overtones.

Yet in the thirteenth and fourteenth centuries one senses a change in the air. If Matthew Paris does only use the word once, he nonetheless uses it in a strikingly full sense. In a paragraph which notes the damage to Christendom of Louis IX's sudden return to France from the Holy Land, we find that the writer attributes to the ambitions of Countess Margaret of Flanders the 'disturbed state of almost the whole of Europe'.[7] The chronicler Higden describes the city of Paris as 'flourishing in Europe

[1] *Chronica Major*, ed. Luard, R.S., v. 439, (below, n. 7).
[2] See above, p. 42.
[3] Ed. P. Paris, 6 vols., Paris 1836-8, i. 9, ii. 35-6, iii. 365.
[4] *Ibid.*, ii. 203, iii. 204, 372, 388, 389, 397, v. 101, vi. 386; cf. iv. 86, v. 99.
[5] *Ibid.*, iii. 400.
[6] *Ibid.*, iv. 255.
[7] Above, n. 1: 'Ecce jam fere tota Europa pro luxuria muliebri est commota', (s.a. 1254).

as Athens of old in Greece'.[1] For Dante writing at the turn of the thirteenth and fourteenth centuries the word is fairly rare, but has relevance beyond that of mere description: 'Italy is the finest part of Europe' he says in the *De Monarchia*[2]; the fame of the Malespini is known 'throughout Europe', he writes in the *Purgatory*[3]; while in that remarkable philological work, *De vulgari eloquentia* he is really attempting an analysis of European language.[4] There are occasions, then, when Dante resorts to the word because he finds it useful[5]; the other moments in which we find it in his work are hardly more numerous.[6] When we come to the next generation of Florentine scholarship and poetry the scene is transformed. One can count the score or so of references to Europe in Dante: in Petrarch they are too frequent for enumeration. There are as many instances of the word in the 'Familiar Letters' of Petrarch as there are in the whole of Dante, and the word is given its full sense: for long there have been no wars in Europe comparable in ferocity to the Anglo-French conflict[7]; who is as celebrated in Italy—nay in Europe—as King Robert[8]; Venice is the most splendid city which Petrarch has seen, and he has seen almost all those that matter in Europe[9]; and so on.[10]

Moreover in some of the authors we have mentioned there is more than a hint that in using 'Europe' they intended something akin to the sense we have associated with 'Christendom'. Consider Dante arguing against the notion that the Church conferred temporal power on the emperor. The church has not the power to do this from

---

[1] R.S., i. 272: 'Ibi floret civitas Parisius ... ita refulgens in Europa, sicut Athenae quondam in Gracia'. And cf. the following sentence, quoted above, p. 49.

[2] *De Mon.*, II. iii. 16.   [3] *Purg.*, VIII. 123.

[4] Esp. see *De Vulg. Eloqu.*, I. viii. 5-6.   [5] And see below.

[6] See *Opere di Dante*, ed. M. Barbi *et al.*, Florence 1921, index by M. Casella, s.n. 'Europa'.

[7] *Le familiari*, ed. V. Rossi and U. Bosco, Edizione nazionale, 4 vols., Florence 1933-42, III. x. 2.   [8] IV. ii. 7.   [9] VIII. v. 14.

[10] IX. xiii. 17; XV. vii. 12-16; XVIII. i. 18; XVIII. ii. 2; XXI. viii. 22; XXII. xiv. 64; cf. X. i. 15. See further below, p. 60.

any general consent of mortals, he says, for 'not only do Asians and Africans reject this notion, but even most natives of Europe do so too'.[1] The 'even' here surely indicates that both church and empire are rooted in Europe in a way which made the continent different from the other two. A rather similar implication lies behind a gloomy survey of the contemporary political scene in one of Petrarch's letters: England and France are at war with each other; in Germany and Italy there are civil disturbances; and so—after references to other areas such as the islands of the Mediterranean and Greece—to the conclusion 'in the rest of Europe Christ is either unknown or unloved'. 'I shall keep silent' he goes on 'about Asia and Africa' though we know they were once provinces of Christ.[2] Here again the force of the passage depends on an assumption that Europe and Christendom are virtually one. And this surely lies behind odd expressions in the *Grandes Chroniques de France*: we read on one occasion of the defeat of the Christian forces by 'Les Turs', to the detriment of 'overseas Christendom' (la crestienté d'outremer)[3]; on another occasion Acre is described as 'a refuge and aid for Christendom in those overseas areas'.[4] After all, an earlier generation would have regarded the Syrian coast as being an integral part of Christendom. Another fourteenth-century writer, this time an Englishman, also implies an awareness of this: Europe, says the *Cursor Mundi*, was the third part of the world, which fell to Japheth; today it has in it most of the Christian kingdoms.[5]

These hints and suggestions will form the theme of

[1] '... cum non modo Asiani et Affricani omnes, quin etiam major pars Europam colentium hoc abhorreat', *De Mon.*, III. xiv. 7; on this sentence see further below, p. 86.

[2] '... in reliquis Europe Cristus vel incognitus vel invisus est ... Taceo Asiam totam atque Africam etc.', *Le familiari*, XV. vii. 14-15.

[3] iii. 372.

[4] 'Acre la cité qui estoit le recours et l'aide de crestienté en ycelles parties d'outre-mer', *Grandes Chroniques*, v. 99.

[5] E.E.T.S., i. 130: 'It [Europe] hatt quar mast to day
    Regns o þe cristen lay.'

this chapter and the next in which an attempt will be made to show that in the fourteenth and fifteenth centuries forces were at work which tended towards an identification of Europe and Christendom, that contemporaries became aware of this and began to adjust their vocabulary to a new situation.

There were, in fact, a good many reasons why a fresh attitude might be provoked to the larger questions of social unities. Earlier universal bodies, the church and, to an even greater degree, the empire, were weakening and in the religious character of the fourteenth-century provincialisms of various kinds were evident. If the Turks were pressing ominously on the confines of Christendom, Christianity was nonetheless extending to cover the whole of the European continent and the unity thus achieved was consolidated by the nature of international trade.

These developments were well under way during the fourteenth century, and in no field is this more evident than in the church. The culmination of the 'Caesaropapism' of earlier ages, the attempt to make the pope a universal prince, was accomplished in the rumbustious pontificate of Boniface VIII (1294-1303). The symbolic significance of the bull *Unam Sanctam*, with its ambitious peroration demanding global obedience to the Holy See, has often been stressed, and so has the prompt reaction of the rulers of Christendom. Boniface VIII's earlier attempt to impose a barrier between the clergy and the taxation of the local king had been resisted by both Philip IV of France and Edward I of England. If the brunt of disputing *Unam Sanctam* fell upon the French king alone, the whole of subsequent history was to show that he was supported by secular princes everywhere. For the emergent Gallicanism of the French church was paralleled by a similar intransigence in England, Spain and Germany. The English sovereigns of the fourteenth century may not have had English popes dwelling on the borders of their territory as the French had French popes at Avignon; but the English church in the reign of Edward III and his successors was obedient to the king as it had never been before. Indeed the king himself was pressed into compliance with an anti-ecclesiastical if not an anti-clerical attitude by the very pronounced opinions of the gentry and nobles in parliament. To these developments in France, England and elsewhere, the papacy—isolated from its main territories in Italy and therefore more dependent than before on financial support from Christendom at large—was completely unable to offer an effective reply. A pathetically small number of clergy were provided to benefices in 'foreign' lands, a few university doctors from 'foreign' lands made a career in the curia or its agencies, but the international character of the church as known in earlier ages was gravely impaired. The chain of papally-appointed strangers who had enriched the English church —Augustine, Lanfranc, Anselm—was by now a thing of the remote past and the handful of non-native prelates we meet in the later middle ages in England were the nominees of the king and were hated by their clerical contemporaries as rapacious interlopers. The curia no longer visibly transcended the frontiers of secular states: it was overwhelmingly French before 1378 as it was overwhelmingly Italian in the fifteenth century and thereafter. From the viewpoint of practical organization and control the Church was already composed of separate churches. That the universities in each country continued to look to the pope is far from being evidence of a lively oecumenical movement: it is the best possible evidence that church preferment was now constricted by the narrow boundaries of lay politics.

Even the ardours and the errors of the fourteenth-century Christian have an oddly parochial appearance if we compare them with the phenomena of the past. We find no fourteenth-century Cluny or Cîteaux; no Bernard or Francis arose to set Christendom afire from end to end. The fourteenth-century saint was, so to speak, a vernacular creation, and the mysticism which pervades so much speculation and devotion in this period is ever tending towards a subjective view-point, just as it is increasingly gravitating to the laity. It was precisely such secular adherents of extravagant religion who engendered the ill-defined errors condemned by the church as Beghardism. We can say with confidence that this type of heresy was also parochial, troubling here a town and there a diocese, but not covering whole provinces like the errors of the Cathari or the Waldensians. The international heresies of the fourteenth century were sterile and academic: John XXII's views on the Beatific Vision stimulated only theologians, and the Franciscan zealots to whom the same pope was obnoxious transgressed *de opinione* and not, as earlier, *de paupere vita*.

If we can assert that the church had gone far to losing its practical identity with Christendom, the other universal power, the empire, may be dismissed more summarily. There had always been an eastern emperor; there were substantial areas of the West which had never formed part of the Latin empire; and even in Germany and Italy the emperors after 1272 were shadows of their predecessors. Italy was never again to be effectively part of the Empire and in Germany the reality of power lay with a number of secular and ecclesiastical princes whose rights were tentatively recognized in 1338 at Rense and were finally consecrated in the Golden Bull of 1356. By divorcing the empire from the papacy the magnates of Germany succeeded in divorcing the empire from Germany itself, in all but name.

One must recognise that the empire played a more positive role in the promotion of political coherence than these remarks suggest. This was, however, on a theoretical plane rather than on a practical one. Legists of all continental countries tended to speculate within a framework which accepted the emperor as *dominus mundi*. The thirteenth century saw the elaboration of a maxim of jurisprudence, 'a king who does not recognise a superior in his kingdom is an emperor', which pays remarkable tribute not only to the independence of kings but also to the notion of empire.[1] This was to provoke an attitude to sovereignty which was undoubtedly a distinguishing common feature of the kingdoms of the West. But for practical purposes it still further limited the empire as an international force. Not only did the French and English kings claim to be emperors in their own lands; even in Italy the civilian lawyers glossed the precepts of Roman Law so as to restrict the autocracy of the emperor. From the fourteenth century the 'empire' was little more than a name for Germany—a Germany where the emperor counted only because, besides being emperor, he was a dynast in his own right. In the later Middle Ages the emperors seldom advanced their claim to universal monarchy.[2]

The church as an international institution had thus had much of its force drained from it by the mid-fourteenth century and so had the empire. Yet the area of Christian territory had expanded by this period to cover almost the whole of the continent. By this time only one area was non-Christian because it had never been Christian— Lithuania. Lithuania was already sandwiched between Orthodox Christian communities in Russia and Latin Christians in Poland and in 1386 was converted by the marriage of the Polish heiress Hedwiga with the Great Prince Jagiello (Wladislaw II). Thus by the end of the century Christianity had penetrated to every corner of Europe. In Spain, which had once been entirely Christian, the Moors were now confined to the small kingdom

[1] F. Calasso, *I glossatori e la teoria della sovranità*, Florence 1945.

[2] For a fourteenth-century example of such a claim see the imperial encyclical of 29 June 1312 in which Henry VII advances the necessity of all men necessarily being in the last resort under one prince, M.G.H., Leg. IV, *Constitutiones* IV, ii (ed. J. Schwalm), p. 802; repeating Dante's arguments in the *Monarchia* (esp. I. viii).

of Granada, which was to fall into Christian hands a century after the conversion of Lithuania.[1] It was also in the second half of the fourteenth century that the grip of the Golden Horde on Russia relaxed and the princes of Moscow began to extend their authority east and south, round and beyond the Don.

If Christians in Europe had been extending the area of their religion, the reverse was true of Christian communities outside Europe. Aside from the invasion of the Mongols which did terrible but temporary damage in Poland, Hungary, Serbia and Bulgaria in the thirteenth century, a more permanent advance against Christendom must be noted. Acre, the last Christian stronghold in Syria, fell in 1291 to the Mamluk rulers of Egypt. This left in Asia only the territory of the Eastern Empire and the tenuous Christian groups of Asia Minor and beyond.

The Eastern Empire was the victim of a steady advance by the Ottoman Turks. From a modest beginning in the reign of Otman (d. 1326) they extended their lands mainly at the expense of Byzantium. In the reign of his successor Orkhan (d. 1360) practically every Greek town south of the Bosphorus had been occupied by the Ottomans. By the end of the century all that remained in Christian hands in Asia Minor were a few coastal towns and the thin strip of Trebizond on the southern shore of the Black Sea, and the isolated town of Philadelphia. As for the Christian churches of Asia,[2] they had for the most part been seriously weakened by the fourteenth century. Armenia, overrun by Egyptian forces in 1373 and later occupied by Ottoman Turks, maintained a church which was divided owing to attempts to achieve union with Rome. Christians in Georgia, to the south of Trebizond, submitted first to Mongol control and then to the Ottomans. The Nestorian Christians, widely scattered in Asia, were

---

[1] Below, p. 81.
[2] See the useful summary in A. S. Atiya, *Crusade in the Later Middle Ages*, London 1938, pp. 269-78.

everywhere in a minority and the thirteenth-century attempts to effect a union between them and the Latins had revealed divergences too deep to be bridged: they too in various ways succumbed to Islam. Finally Christian Abyssinia could preserve its Coptic church secure in its mountain stronghold but was powerless to protect the Christians of Egypt, who were victims of the brutality both of Latin Christians (as in the sack of Alexandria by the 'Crusaders' in 1365) and of the Mamluks.[1] There may have been a time in the thirteenth century when the Tartars looked like uniting Asia and Europe in one vast empire; indeed Christians in the West saw a converted Mongol horde as the instrument of a vast extension of Christendom.[2] This failed, however.[3] And there was never any moment afterwards when Christianity might have again demonstrated the oecumenical character of its earliest centuries. By the fourteenth century Christendom in Asia Minor and further east, like Christendom in Africa, was fragmented, powerless and more or less cut off from the Christian centres of the West. The idea of reunion never died.[4] But it was a chimera only. To the ordinary Christian of the West these fellow Christians of the Orient were a strange collection: 'all their variance were too mickle to tell', wrote Mandeville[5]; they belonged to the marvels and monsters of the traveller's tales.

The Ottoman Turks were not content with the conquest of the Asiatic provinces of Byzantium. Before they had entirely mastered the south shore of the sea of Marmora they had benefited from division in the Eastern Empire to the extent of occupying territory in Thrace. From 1366 Adrianople was the headquarters of Turkish power and by the end of the fourteenth century Ottoman armies had conquered up to the Danube; at the battle of

---

[1] A. S. Atiya, op. cit., 273, 366.
[2] Cf. Roger Bacon, *Opus Majus*, ed. Bridges, i. 266, ii. 376, 387-8.
[3] S. Runciman, *History of the Crusades*, iii. 246, 253-4, 258-60, 293-314.
[4] See further below, p. 82.
[5] *Travels*, ed. M. Letts, Hakluyt Society 1953, i. 85 (ii. 295).

Nicopolis (1396) they had routed the solitary attempt of western Christians to bring substantial relief to Constantinople. This constriction of the Greek empire was not compensated for by the existence in central and eastern Europe of orthodox Christian churches, for these would not admit obedience to the Byzantine patriarch. At just about the same time as the Crusaders were routed at Nicopolis, the patriarch Antony had to rebuke the Grand Duke Basil I of Moscow for his assertion of ecclesiastical independence: 'the doctrine of one oecumenical emperor had never been laid down more forcibly or with more fiery eloquence'.[1] Events were not to give much more time for the expression of this consciousness of proud superiority.

In a totally different way homogeneity was being lent to Latin Christendom. This was in the sphere of economic activity. Roman trade had—like Roman government—been inter-continental, even if on a relatively modest scale. Medieval trade was primarily confined to traffic in the products of the West. Certainly the Orient and Africa contributed important quantities of rare commodities—gold, spices and chemicals. But the bulk of even luxury goods—fine cloth, fine metal work, *objets d'art*—were produced in western workshops, while the enormous exchange upon which mercantile prosperity directly depended was in cereals, wines, wool, salt, fish, timber and stone. It used to be argued that the Crusades, by providing a direct link between Italian ports and Asia Minor, were the main stimulus to the growth of international commerce. This now seems less likely: the extraordinary efflorescence of mercantile activity in the eleventh and twelfth centuries was more probably a reflection of a thousand minor centres of economic life, themselves responding to an agrarian expansion deriving from a steadily increased population. However that may be, there is no denying that until the end of the thirteenth

[1] Ostrogorsky, 491-2.

century the rapidly developing economy of Christendom was in a very genuine sense framed within the limits of the Atlantic in the West, the Baltic in the North, the rivers running between the Baltic and the Black Sea, and the long southern channel of the Mediterranean.[1] Even the recession of the fourteenth century was circumscribed in this way: the long periods of famine and the recurrent waves of Black Death were essentially European phenomena—which passed as uninfluential in other areas where both plague and famine were endemic.

The pressures we have briefly outlined in the preceding pages weakened the old international or Christian categories, yet brought about an increasingly obvious unity to the European scene. They were to be greatly intensified in the last quarter of the fourteenth and the first half of the fifteenth centuries. If for a decade after 1401 (when Timurlenk defeated the Ottoman Sultan Bayezid) Turkish pressure on the West was relaxed, the internal contradictions in the universal church produced more divisions than before.

In 1378 occurred a schism the like of which had not been seen earlier. The popes had resided at Avignon more or less continuously since 1305 and when an election to the vacant throne was made necessary by the death of Gregory XI in Rome there was every likelihood that a Frenchman would be elected by the predominantly French college of cardinals. But the Roman crowd, outside the conclave but influential nonetheless, called for an Italian and the conclave elected a relatively obscure Neapolitan as Urban VI. Urban proved of unstable temperament and a violent critic of the cardinals who had elected him. His threats touched the cardinals on a tender spot for they had been anxious for more than a generation to safeguard their rights as against papal autocracy. Within a short space the French cardinals (tamely supported by the

[1] Cf. Y. Renouard, *English Historical Review*, lxix (1954), 88.

Italian minority) withdrew and elected a French pope, Clement VII. The schism thus created was to last until 1417—intensified after 1409 by the existence of a third line of popes, stemming from the Council of Pisa, where cardinals from the Roman and Avignonese obediences met in an attempt to heal the breach.

The brief outline of the origin of the schism given above was necessary to show that national animosities were not primarily responsible for the schism. But once the schism occurred it was exacerbated by national divisions. France supported the French pope, England the pope of Rome; because England was for Rome, Scotland was for Avignon; and so with the rest of Christendom. Princes chose popes as, two centuries earlier, popes sought to choose princes. The rival pontiffs were naturally more dependent than their predecessors on the support of the lay powers of the West, whose effective control of church and clergy was correspondingly increased. Beyond even that, the very notion of an undivided church was the concern rather of the kings of Europe than of the schismatic popes. The administrations of Richard II and Henry IV and Henry V of England, of Charles VI of France negotiated between themselves and with other governments to find a way out of an impasse created by the church itself; it was through the active intervention of the Emperor Sigismund that Spanish support was withdrawn from Benedict XIII and an end made to the schism by the election of Martin V in the imperial city of Constance in 1417.

Bedraggled and compromised by these proceedings, popes for the next century and a half were in practice little more than Italian princelings. But the damage to an ecclesiastical Christendom went deeper than that. The international machinery of the church was seriously impaired, conscientious clergymen embarked on a radical re-examination of the structure of the church, and constitutionally the popes were compelled to recognize *de jure*

F

the longstanding *de facto* power of kings in matters ecclesiastical. These points may be cursorily examined.

The great international orders of the Church had promoted an actively united Christendom. Monks and later friars were often exempt from local ecclesiastical supervision and looked ultimately to the pope, through a hierarchy of provincial and general synods or chapters. Admittedly this organization was working sluggishly in the fourteenth century, the Franciscans in particular being in a state of almost permanent civil war. But the schism dealt a further serious blow. As several of the orders had headquarters in France or in areas subject to Avignon (Cluny, Cîteaux, Carthusians, Premonstratensians, Grandmont), governments 'obedient' to the 'Roman' pope took active steps to discontinue any practical obedience by houses of these orders in their own territories. In England the 'alien' priory, owing duty and some financial dues to a continental mother house, had been a matter of suspicious legislation since 1307: it was virtually extinguished by 1414; and the monks with a French origin were forced to renounce their traditional organization, accepting the province as in practice the largest unit. These developments are found, with variations, elsewhere in Western Europe, both depriving later popes of much influence and precluding much-needed reform. Nothing shows this better than the regional nature of such reforms as were attempted—the so-called 'congregations' or groups of more or less adjacent houses—in the early fifteenth century. As might have been anticipated the Franciscan order carried this provincialization of organization to its greatest limits.

Meanwhile the urgency of the situation provoked much speculation after 1378 into questions of a fundamental kind. If the undivided church owed allegiance to a single head and yet found itself divided into two under two heads, where in reality lay the unity of the church? The answers given at the time to this question are complicated. But they may not unfairly be summarised by saying that it was generally agreed that the church was a mystical union of all Christians. This on the face of it was merely a return to ideas prevalent before the sovereignty of the popes had created a visible sign of unity, and for our purposes it is more to the point to note that reforming thought attempted to express the position practically by a conciliar structure: in the last resort the pope was amenable to a council in which the church might achieve as nearly as possible the reflection of the will of all believers and thus of Christ. Legislation to this effect was passed by the Council of Constance and Christians generally assumed that it had been accepted by the pope. That it was not so, that later popes successfully disputed and invalidated the doctrine of conciliar supremacy, is less important than that the attempt had been made to express constitutionally the notion of a 'mixed government' for the church.

Kings benefited, as we have noted, from the schism itself. Their gains were consolidated by the manner in which the schism was ended. At Constance a number of 'national' concordats were approved which were the tangible expression, not only of a failure to reach agreement on general reform, but of the practical separation of the great kingdoms from an ecclesiastical point of view. The Gallican liberties now begin to acquire a form, and a series of concordats in France show how the royal power of controlling the church in all but its spiritual aspects was carried forward. In England the concordat after Constance was not of much significance, so insulated from papal interference were the English clergy by earlier royal actions. Above all, in Germany the local prince and the local prelate came to terms and throughout the fifteenth and sixteenth centuries evinced an attachment to 'conciliarism' which, if defended as an instrument of reform, was also most certainly popular because of a desire to remove the vestiges of Roman power.

Deprived in these ways of most of its unifying significance, the church was no longer the engine of Christendom. Fourteenth- and fifteenth-century popes were unable to rouse Christians to the Crusade, while the outlying
Asiatic portions of Christendom were dwindling to
nothing. Christendom, in short, was being confined to
Europe and yet being deprived of its *raison d'être*—the
concept of a dynamic church under papal leadership.
Christian as never before, displaying (for all their diver-
sity) forms of political association which marked it off
sharply from Asia and Africa, maintained by economic
relations which bound the continent together in both
prosperity and plague, Europe by the fifteenth century
was already a unity in fact. We shall see in the next
chapter how the consciousness of this gradually made
itself felt.

CHAPTER 5

THE EMERGENCE OF EUROPE

THE use, and the emotional content, of the word Europe significantly increased in the fourteenth and especially in the fifteenth centuries. The occasions for this derived, at any rate indirectly, from some of the matter discussed in the previous chapter. The residence of the popes at Avignon, the problem of reform and the constitution of the Council of Constance all produced developments relevant to our enquiry. Other factors to be considered in this chapter are: the influence of humanist literary attitudes, the fall of Constantinople as a challenge to Christian Europe, and the influence of new types of cartography.

Many earnest Christians in the fourteenth century were distressed by the prolonged papal residence outside Italy. The bishop of Rome should have more than a nominal connection with his see; residence in Italy would clear the papacy from compromising associations with France; it would also go far to bring back prosperity to the city of Rome itself and good order to Italy as a whole.[1] No one conducted a more vigorous campaign against the residence of the popes at Avignon than the Florentine exile, Petrarch. In 1366 he published a letter claiming that only the crudest motives retained pope and cardinals in the Rhône valley.[2] From this point a lively controversy developed between Petrarch and a series of French apologists

---

[1] In general see G. Mollat, *Les papes d'Avignon*, 9th ed., Paris 1949, pp. 249-74.
[2] *Sen.*, VII. i (29 June 1366). Long extracts from this letter are printed by A. F. Johnson, *F. Petrarchae Epistolae Selectae*, Oxford 1923, pp. 160-9.

for Avignon.[1] The exchanges were scarcely edifying and much turned on Petrarch's accusation that the French were barbarians, like all other trans-Alpine peoples, and counter charges of corruption and incivility in Italy: all a curious anticipation of the later battle of the books which developed between the two countries in the sixteenth century. The case for the pope's return to Italy was, indeed, difficult to controvert and the French writers were hard put to it to find arguments for a headquarters of the church in southern France. One French writer, however, found an ingenious line of defence. The anonymous writer of a tract which comes towards the end of the pamphlet war prefers Avignon to Rome on geographical grounds of a kind which must attract our attention:

The case for Avignon is established by the very situation of the place, which is more equidistant from the modern boundaries of the Catholic church, and whence our lord the pope may for ever administer to the Christian faithful his spiritual medicine with more ease and equity.[2]

The writer goes on to stress that for the same reason the sending out of legates and the determination of causes reserved to the pope will be facilitated.[3] At much the same time a delegation from the French court placed before Urban V all the arguments that could be mustered against the pope's return to Italy. Among these we find some points similar to those made above. The author (Ancel Choquart) makes two premises towards the end of his long address: that Europe is one of the three parts

[1] This is fairly fully surveyed by Enrico Cocchia, 'Magistri I. de Hysdinio invectiva contra Fr. Petrarcham et Fr. Petrarchae contra cuiusdam Galli calumnias apologia', *Atti della Reale Accademia di Archeologia, Lettere e belli arti*, Naples, new series VII. i (1920), 92-103; Hesdin's work is printed pp. 112-39, and Petrarch's reply pp. 140-202.

[2] H. Cochin, 'La grande controverse de Rome et d'Avignon au XIVe siècle', *Études Italiennes*, Paris, iii (1921), 1-14, 83-94, prints this treatise. The original runs: Hanc rem situs probat loci, distantis plus equaliter a finibus modernis ecclesie catholice, unde potest facilius et equabilius impertiri dominus noster papa suam spiritalem [sic] medicinam cristianis agentibus perpetualiter.

[3] He adds, too, that Avignon is nearer to the scholars of Paris than Rome is.

of the world, the inheritance of Japheth, and situated between North and East; and that 'these days Christians
dwell in Europe—for none or very few Christian princes
rule outside Europe'. But the geographers demonstrate
that the centre of Europe is Marseilles, reckoning the
length and breadth of Christian territory less Greece,
which is schismatic. Now Christ's vicar should dwell in
the midst of Christendom: Christ lived and died in the
centre of the earth; afterwards Rome was chosen because
at the time it was centrally situated; now it is Marseilles.
In any case, where the Pope is, there is Rome.[1]

What is arresting in these guileless productions is the
reference in the first to the 'modern boundaries of the
Catholic Church', and in the second to 'present-day
Christians dwelling in Europe'. Rome as the centre of a
Mediterranean church was clearly well-placed. But now
the church no longer radiates out over the lands formerly
in the Roman empire. Its frontiers have contracted to a
point where Avignon (or Marseilles) can seem more
central than Rome. There is no doubt that in fact the
writers of the treatises had some right on their side, and
that others besides Frenchmen saw Christendom in the
same light.

In 1407 an Englishman also argued that France was

[1] This extraordinary effusion is printed by C. E. Du Boulay, *Historia
Universitatis Parisiensis*, 1665-1673, iv. 396-412, where it is attributed to
Nicholas Oresme. On the authorship and occasion see Mollat, *Papes d'Avignon*,
p. 253. Du Boulay's text is very bad and in quoting it I have not attempted to
emend it. The relevant passages are on pp. 409-10: 'Praeterea supponendum
est quod divisa tota terra habitabili in 3 partes, scilicet Asiam et Europam, quae
scilicet Europa situatur inter Septentrionem et Occidens, ipsa cessit in partem
... Iaphet ... Supponendum est quod prope istam Europam habitant his
temporibus Christiani. Unde nulli vel pauci Principes Christiani dominantur
extra Europam.... Item sciendum est quod non urbs Roma sed Massilia est
in medio praefatae Europae situata ... consideratis longitudinibus et latitudin-
ibus Civitatem Christianorum dempta Graecia quae hodie est schismatica.
Ergo ut sicut Christus tenet sedem suam ... in medio Christianitatis, ita et
papa eius vicarius hoc idem facere debet.... Christus Salvator noster in medio
terrae habitavit in terris et ibi mortuus. Postea Roma quae media Christianorum pro tunc fuit electa ... scilicet de Marsilia quae est locus medius ut est
dictum.... Nec Roma sibi causare potest aliquid detractum, quia ubi papa,
ibi Roma et apostolorum limina.' Praise of the university of Paris precedes
this.

now at the centre of the Christian world. This was Richard Young, who was translated from Bangor to Rochester in the very year that he tendered advice to the curia on how to end the schism. His suggestion was a general council, not in itself a very novel proposal. Such a meeting France, the prime supporter of the 'Avignon' papacy, could be compelled to attend under threat of being otherwise delivered over to the spoliation of other Christian powers.[1] He considered that in fact the French would comply and not prevaricate—'as the Greeks always do: after all the Greeks are on the very edge of Christendom, whereas the French are at the very heart of it'.[2] An English acceptance of the central position of France is even better evidence than the pamphlet of Petrarch's French critic that such a view was generally held. It was with difficulty that Englishmen admitted France to be at the heart of anything that mattered.

By the time that the council for which Young had argued finally met the schism had lasted more than a generation and was provoking desperation among many. 'The pagan world can exclaim "Christendom is finished",' wrote a French publicist in 1399; 'one tongue hates another tongue, each nation its neighbour.'[3] These divisions had to be solved if a permanent reform was to be accomplished, yet the very fact that national differences were reflected in the Council of Constance proved a stumbling block to progress. Speculation on both reform and on national differences contributed, however, to a clearer view of the society of Christian nations.

[1] 'Spoliis Christi fidelium', Martène et Durand, *Amplissima collectio*, vii. 749. For the identity of the author see E. F. Jacob, *Essays in the Conciliar Epoch*, 2nd ed., Manchester 1953, p. 71.
[2] 'Prout faciunt Graeci, quia illi quasi in extremitatibus Christianitatis, isti vero in corde et medio Christianorum existunt', Martène et Durand, *loc. cit.*
[3] ' "Finis christianorum"! nunc exclamat paganitas. ... Lingua aliam linguam detestatur ex ea, et natio sibi nationem proximam', H. Bonet, *Somnium super materia scismatis*, in I. Arnold's ed. of *L'Apparicion maistre Jehan de Meun*, Paris, 1926, p. 106.

This may be seen first of all in the scope of some of the proposals to make the college of cardinals a more or less representative body, so that when its members acted as papal counsellors and above all when they elected a pope they would reflect the general views of the church at large, viewed as it was as fundamentally the mystical assembly of all Christians.[1] Such devices acquired a sudden actuality when the Council turned to elect a pope in 1417 and in one of the memoranda drawn up at that time we are sharply confronted with a picture of Christendom very distinct from that discussed in Chapter 2 above, very close to the views of the French opponent of Petrarch and of Richard Young. If the election of a pope on this occasion were to be in the hands of the cardinals (predominantly French and Italian) together with an even representation of all the 'nations' at Constance (Italian, French, English, German and Spanish), this would tip the scales in favour of the Italians and French. So said the German nation.[2] The Italians and French comprised less than half of Christendom, while the German and English nations constituted 'a half of all Christendom or thereabouts'.[3] To reckon dioceses as the units comprising Christendom was ludicrous since they are so ill-distributed: Italy has more than the rest of Christendom put together, yet is in reality scarcely the quarter of Christendom.[4] Behind this unbalance lies the loss of massive Christian territories. Of the twelve areas converted by the twelve apostles, eleven are schismatic or heretical.[5]

The notion that Christendom has changed its boundaries is also revealed in an earlier and perhaps more significant episode at Constance. The original 'nations', into which the council was divided for deliberative purposes, were based on those found in the big arts faculties

[1] Above, p. 71.
[2] H. Finke, *Acta Concilii Constanciencis*, 4 vols. 1896–1928, iii. 632.
[3] *Ibid.*, p. 633: 'Germanorum et Anglicorum nationes, que . . . medietatem totius Christianitatis continent vel quasi.'
[4] *Ibid.*, pp. 636–7.　　　　　　　　　　　　[5] *Ibid.*, pp. 628–9.

at universities, the practice of Paris being most influential. To the Italian, French, English and German nations, thus established, was added in 1416 the Spanish nation. The problem then arose: were the Spanish delegates to be formed into a fifth nation or should they constitute a part of an existing nation?

The matter was hardly discussed on its merits, for the French—victims of successful English aggression in the campaigns of Henry V—seized on the opportunity to attack England at Constance.[1] Basing their case primarily on the general plausibility of having four nations rather than five, the French nation sought to reinforce their case by invoking the quadripartite division of Christendom implicit in Benedict XII's bull *Vas electionis* of 1336.[2] This pronouncement had, in fact, the aim only of regulating the collection of certain papal taxes, notably procurations. For this purpose the bull had grouped together the following areas:

I. France, Navarre, Majorca, Dauphiné, Savoy, Provence, Forcalquier.
II. Germany, Hungary, Bohemia, Poland, Norway, Denmark, England, Scotland, Sweden.
III. Castile, Leon, Aragon and Portugal and dependencies of their sovereigns except Sardinia and Corsica.
IV. The provinces of Italy, Sclavonia, Greece, Cyprus, 'and the other kingdoms and islands; and all provinces and areas overseas and even beyond the seas'.[3]

In claiming, despite the terms of the bull, the small size

[1] The order of events may be followed in Fillastre's 'Journal', Finke ii. 82, 90, 99-100; see also M. Creighton, *History of the Papacy*, London 1897, ii. 80-1; N. Valois, *La France et le grand schisme*, Paris 1896-1902, iv. 376; Louise R. Loomis, 'Nationality at the Council of Constance', *American Historical Review*, xliv (1939), 508-27, esp. 522-6.

[2] *Extravagantes Communes*, iii, tit. X. Cf. Mollat, *op. cit.*, 509. A quotation from the bull forms part of doc. no. 502 in W. E. Lunt, *Papal Revenues in the Middle Ages*, New York 1934, ii. 430.

[3] 'Et caeteris Regnis, Insulisque, et aliis Provinciis et partibus omnibus ultramarinis et etiam transmarinis'.

of their delegation and the modest domains of their kingdom, that they should constitute a nation, the English were claiming to be a fifth of Christendom: a deplorable step in the view of the French.[1]

To this the English replied in a broadside which denied the fourfold division as advanced by the French and argued strongly in favour of the superior eminence, antiquity and power of the English king and kingdom.[2] Science taught that the earth had three parts, Asia, Africa and Europe and that Europe was divided into four empires—the Roman, the Byzantine, the Irish (now transferred to the English) and the Spanish.[3] The papal obedience in Europe must correspond with the four divisions in Albertus Magnus—an Eastern Church, a Western, a Northern and a Southern:

> The Eastern region or Christian church owing obedience to the pope in Europe comprises Hungary, Bohemia, Poland and Germany. The Western part or church is France or Spain. The Northern part or church in Europe as a whole is England, Wales, Scotland and Ireland (with their islands), Denmark, Sweden and Norway. The Southern is Italy and those of the Greeks in our obedience—that is to say the Cypriots and the Cretans in Candia.[4]

This was a natural division. Other principles of division (such as language or rulers) would produce an unwieldy multiplicity of units; divisions according to wealth or political influence would be forever changing, while the pride of nations would not suffer hierarchies of such a kind. If it be objected that the proposal concentrated on the church in Europe, there were many councils in the

---

[1] Mansi, *Amplissima collectio*, 1759-98, xxvii, col. 1025. (The French protest as a whole is in cols. 1022-31.)   [2] Mansi, xxvii, cols. 1058-70.

[3] 'Europa in quatuor dividitur regna. Primum videlicet Romanum, secundum Constantinopolitanum, tertium regnum Hiberniae, quod iam translatum est in Anglicos, et quartum regnum Hispaniae', col. 1065.

[4] 'Orientalis vero plaga, sive Ecclesia Christianitatis obedientiae papalis in Europa est Hungaria, Bohemia, Polonia et Alemania; Occidentalis etian pars, sive Ecclesia est Francia sive Hispania; Aquilonaris sive septentrionalis pars sive Ecclesia totius Europae est Anglia, Wallia, Scotia et Hybernia cum earum insulis, Dacia, Svecia, Norvegia; Meridionalis est Italia, et si qui Graeci sunt de obedientia nostra, puta Cyprii, et Cretenses in Candia', cols. 1066-7.

past which reflect such a geographical division between East and West.[1]

In thus recalling at the end of their memorandum that there might be more to the church than Europe, the English were being somewhat academic. The whole Anglo-French argument, in fact, revolved round the countries of Europe, and not of a Christendom actually or potentially larger than this. But even the English had no real illusions on the point. An anonymous English draft, which must have been considered by the English delegates at Constance before they issued their formal reply to the French, has survived and is explicit on the point: 'We can prove the fourfold division thus,' says the *Advisamenta*, 'for now only Europe is Christian, and so the fourfold division of the Church is established.'[2] Yet it is significant that the argument is not included in the case officially submitted to the Council. To say in so many words that only Europe was Christian was obviously a difficult thing to do. And the clumsiness of the terminology in the official English submission, where 'region', 'part', 'church' are used as synonymous terms, equally indicates that we are seeing the emergence of a novel notion which strained traditional modes of thought. The fathers of Constance did unquestionably use the phrases we have become familiar with—'Christian people, all the faithful, the flock of Christ, Christians, the peoples of Christendom' and so on.[3] But they were faced, as some

---

[1] Cols. 1067-70.

[2] Von Der Hardt, *Mag. Oec. Conc. Constancience*, 1696-1700, v. 102-3: 'Hoc sic probatur. Qui ex quo sola Europa modo est Christiana, tunc ejus divisio secundum quatuor plagas terrae satis patet.' The debate between the French and English delegates at Constance, including the 'advisamenta', was found by Sir Robert Wingfield on a visit to Constance and published by him at Louvain in 1517 under the title *Nobilissima disceptatio super dignitate et magnitudine regnorum Britannici et Gallici habita ab utriusque oratoribus et legatis in concilio Constantiensi*: Richardus Lepidus Bartholinus (on whom see Allen, *Op. Ep. Erasmi*, ii. 498) contributed a letter to Wingfield. I have been unable to locate a copy of the *editio princeps* and I have used a reprint (J. Adamson, London 1690) in the Signet Library, Edinburgh.

[3] Here, e.g., are the expressions to be found in vol. i of Finke's collection:

of them realized, with a Christendom which was equivalent to no more than Europe, indeed to rather less than the whole of the continent.

In one other field the Council of Constance saw a significant criticism of the older attitudes. The conversion of Lithuania in 1386[1] had deprived the crusading order of eastern Europe, the Teutonic Knights, of their *raison d'être*. Masters of Prussia and of much of the Baltic coastal lands up to the Gulf of Finland, they had preyed not only on pagan Lithuanians but also on Christian Poles. Now that their work could no longer be defended as a crusade a bitter polemic between the Order and the new Poland-Lithuania was carried on and was brought before the Council. Part of the dispute lay in the doctrine of tyrannicide advanced by the Order's propagandist, Falkenberg; this was a problem akin to that discussed in the concurrent debate over the Burgundian apologist, Jean Petit, and need not concern us here.[2] What is relevant is the *Demonstratio* of the Pole, Paulus Vladimiri of Brudzén, rector of Cracow university.[3] In this short but trenchant document,[4] Vladimiri sought to destroy the right of Christians to war upon non-Christians, including pagans. Though (as Vladimiri pointed out) canonists had been cautious in discussing the Christian's right forcibly to dispossess the infidel, moralists and crusading propagandists had not, and the argument of the *Demonstratio* was thus an outright attack on the idea of the Crusade. The Reconquista in Spain was a special case, said Vladimiri; there the Christians were recovering what they once had legally possessed. And Jerusalem was also a special case, for obvious reasons. But for the rest, 'it is not lawful to compel the infidel by force or oppression to become a Christian'.[5]

populus Christianus, omnes Christi fideles, grex christi, Christicolae, christianitatis gentes; in Italian, i veri fideli Christiani, tutti i Christiani.

[1] Above, p. 64. [2] Finke, iv. 237-432.
[3] On the Poles at Constance see *Cambridge History of Poland*, i (1950), pp. 219-20. [4] Von der Hardt, iii. 10-27.
[5] 'Non est licitum, infideles armis vel oppressionibus ad fidem compellere Christianam', *ibid.*, 20.

This position was far from being generally acceptable to the fathers at Constance, though they were in general sympathetic to the plight of the Poles and Lithuanians. But it was much more vehement and wider in its scope than earlier attacks on the notion of the crusades.[1]

The years that followed the end of the Council of Constance were full of further trials for Christendom. The church was divided once more as a fierce struggle developed between the papacy and the Council of Basle, a struggle which did not finally end until 1449. Europe was full of wars, of which the most serious remained the Anglo-French struggle. From the late 1420s the tide of war went against the English; but they refused to admit defeat and France was hardly strengthened, nor Christian unity increased, when the duke of Burgundy in 1435 withdrew his support from his former English ally. In eastern Europe the pressure of the Ottoman Turks was steadily maintained and the facts of the case were hardly obscured by the 'unions' accomplished by Pope Eugenius IV with the Greek Church and other oriental communions. Salonika fell in 1430 and nothing seemed likely to save Constantinople, for the not unsuccessful campaigns of the Venetians by sea and of John Hunyadi on land were defensive in character. To some 1452 seemed a hopeful year for abandoning the 'civil war' in the West and rallying to the defence of eastern Europe: the schism was over, fighting had died down in Germany and in France. So said Jean Germain, bishop of Chalon, when advocating a crusade to Charles VII of France. He again catalogued all the miseries of 'le douloureux estat de Chrestienté'; he again noted that it was the European countries that were 'tous encores au jourd'uy, la Dieu grace, subgectes à Jhesu-crist'; and that all the rest of the world

[1] Palmer A. Throop, *Criticism of the Crusade*, Amsterdam 1940, surveys the discussion down to the end of the thirteenth century. Advocates of peaceful conversion were notably more vocal in the thirteenth century than they had been earlier. Among the most vigorous was Roger Bacon. Throop, pp. 105-12, 120-35 and esp. pp. 111, 133.

had been Christianized by the apostles but was now lost, 'tournée à confusion et totale désolacion'; and—like all other fourteenth- and fifteenth-century advocates of crusade—he also was unsuccessful.[1] The Anglo-French war which had done so much to distract the West from a Crusade petered out in the autumn of 1453, six months after the fall of Constantinople.[2]

There was no acuter observer of these events than Aeneas Sylvius Piccolomini. Born in 1405, he rose in the late 1430s and 1440s by virtue of his skill as a writer and diplomat, until in 1447 he became bishop of Trieste, being translated to Siena in 1450 and elevated to the cardinalate in 1456. He knew France, Scotland, England at first hand, but above all was familiar with Germany and Italy. When he became pope in 1458 as Pius II he was in the best possible position to know the troubled Christian scene and felt acutely his responsibilities.[3] The chief of these he conceived to be the combating of the Turkish menace both by force of persuasion and by force of arms. The voluminous documentation of his pontificate enables us to determine fairly closely what it was, in geographical terms, that Pius II felt was threatened. This was unquestionably Europe.

In his letter to Mahomet, conqueror of Constantinople, Pius lists the 'power of the Christian people'[4]:

We cannot believe that you are unaware of the resources of the Christian people—how strong in Spain, how warlike France, how

---

[1] Ch. Schefer, 'Discours de Jean Germain . . . au roi Charles VII en 1452', *Revue de l'Orient Latin*, Paris, iii (1895), pp. 303-42 and esp. pp. 315, 319, 324, 331.

[2] A recent survey of the period of Ottoman attack will be found in D. M. Vaughan, *Europe and the Turk*, Liverpool 1954, pp. 42-64.

[3] The study by G. Voigt, 3 vols., Berlin 1856-63, remains basic. There are lives in English by W. Boulting (1908) and C. M. Ady (1913); there is a recent study in Italian by G. Paparelli, Naples 1950.

[4] Pio II, *Lettera a Maometto II*, ed. G. Toffanin, Naples 1953, p. 110: 'Nos non ita ignarum te credimus nostrarum rerum, quin scias quanta est Christianae gentis potentia, quam valida Hispania, quam bellicosa Gallia, quam populosa Germania, quam fortis Britannia, quam audax Polonia, quam strenua Hungaria quam dives et animosa et bellicarum perita rerum Italia.'

numerous are the people of Germany, how powerful Britain, how bold Poland, how vigorous Hungary, how rich, spirited and skilled in warfare is Italy.

This is, in fact, a catalogue not of Christian peoples, but of European Christian peoples. Pius was explicit in rejecting the argument that Mahomet in fact controlled Christians in his domains, for these are written off as not true Christians:

> They are all tainted with error, despite their worship of Christ— Armenians, Jacobites, Maronites and the rest. The Greeks fell away from union with the Roman church when you invaded Constantinople. They had still refused to accept the settlement achieved at Florence and remained in error.[1]

For Europe and Christendom are identified by the pope: or rather, Christendom is seen as radiating out from a European base. The Turk, says Pius, is sure to heal differences between Western Christian kingdoms if they learn of his approach to *the interior of Christendom*'.[2] Equally, if the Islamic sovereign were to end this most fearful war by accepting conversion, Pius promises him the admiration 'of all Greece, of all Italy, of all Europe' —of the Christian world, in short.[3]

The pope had to contend with another problem. As we have seen, the notion that the Turks were of Trojan descent was widely diffused and the career of this myth was by no means hindered by a profound hostility to the Greeks, not on political or even on religious grounds (for the battered and tiny state had no military force and had had to admit the primacy of Rome) but on ideological grounds. Petrarch had combated the evils of Greek thought as he saw them applied or misapplied by the

---

[1] *Ibid.*, p. 113: 'Omnes aliquo sunt errore imbuti, quamvis Christum colant: Armeni, Jacobitae, Maronei et alia quaedum nomina. Graeci a Romanae ecclesiae unitate aberant, cum tu Constantinopolim invasisisti, neque adhuc decretum Florentinum acceperant et in errore stabant.'

[2] *Ibid.*, p. 111: 'unientur Christiani omnes, siquando te audiant *interiora Christianitatis accedere*'; the same phrase in the bull of 1463: Raynaldus-Baronius, x. 356b.

[3] *Ibid.*, p. 176: 'sic te omnis Graecia, omnis Italia, omnis Europa demirabitur'.

PLATE III. 'The Drunkenness of Noah', from H. Schedel, *Liber Chronicarum*. See p. 103 and n. 2.

schoolmen.[1] In the next century, when many more Greek scholars were on Italian soil, the tension mounted, Aeneas Sylvius himself recounting with pleasure a debate in 1438 when the Latins, victors of old over the Greeks, could now claim to have overcome them in 'science and every branch of scholarship.'[2] Yet the kinship of Turks and Franks might go far to weakening the pope's crusading plans and he consequently argued forcibly against the legend, attributing it solely to the Turks having occupied the land on which Troy was built.[3]

The same assumptions coloured Pius's diplomatic activity, from the ill-starred congress at Mantua in 1459 to the abortive attempt to lead a crusade in person in 1464. At Mantua the resolve was taken, not to recapture the Holy Place, but 'to drive the Turk out of Europe'.[4] 'Give us victory,' the pope prayed in 1463, 'over thine enemies that, having at length recovered Greece, we may sing thy praises through the whole of Europe.'[5] In this strategy the Christians of Asia were hardly regarded as offering more than a possible diversion: they would rise in Asia merely to facilitate the attack to be mounted in Europe against the Turk.[6] Europe, indeed, seemed very much at stake, for in 1461 Trebizond, the only remaining territory under Christian control in Asia Minor, fell to the Ottomans. And it was in the pontificate of Pius II that the infidel took the remaining fragments of Christian Greece—the despotat of the Morea.

---

[1] De sui et aliorum ignorantia, ed. L. M. Capelli, Paris 1906.

[2] R. Sabbadini, Storia del Ciceronianismo, Turin 1885, pp. 81-2.

[3] Joly, op. cit., 527n. The fanciful genealogies of the Turks themselves, tracing their origin to Noah, were adapted to the process which the pope deplored: cf. P. Wittek, The Rise of the Ottoman Empire, (Royal Asiatic Society) London 1938, p. 7f.

[4] Raynaldus-Baronius, x. 281a: ' . . . in dieta Mantuana . . . decrevimus, ut Turchum de Europa divino adjutorio fugaremus'. Pius's own considered views on this may be seen in his Commentaries, books ii and iii (ed. F. A. Gragg and L. C. Gabel), Smith College Studies in History, xxv, Northampton, Mass., 1939-40.

[5] Ibid., 362a: 'Da nobis victoriam de tuis hostibus, ut tandem recuperata Graecia, per totam Europam dignas tibi cantemus laudes.'

[6] Ibid., 257b, 258a.

G

The works of Pius II, both before and after his elevation to the papal throne, are full of the use of the word Europe and it would be tedious to rehearse examples.[1] But one point must be insisted on: he turned the word into an adjective. There was little classical encouragement for a use of 'European': *Europaeus* and *Europensis* are found, but not commonly or in the most admired authors. As we have seen there is an isolated case of 'Europeans' being employed by a writer of the eighth century,[2] but his example does not seem to have been followed by later writers. Dante, for instance, goes out of his way to avoid the word in a passage where he writes of 'Asians and Africans' but styles the natives of the third continent as 'inhabitants of Europe'.[3] Even more telling evidence that the adjective was not in common use comes from Boccaccio. In his *Commentary on Dante* Boccaccio has occasion (Purg., xiv. 94) to discuss Crete in relation to the traditional arrangement of continents and seas. He says: 'as the sea which lies towards Africa we call African, so this one we call Europic, which extends to the Island of Crete, where we say that the Aegean Sea ends'.[4] 'Europaic' was not the form that the adjective was to take in Italian (Europeo) or in any vernacular save German; and the only parallel in medieval Latin sources which I have found is in Balbi's *Catholicon*, where it is given as an alternative form (*europicus*) to *europius*.[5] Presumably Boccaccio coined the vernacular word in order to establish that 'thus

[1] On Pius II's attitude to Europe see Werner Fritzemeyer, *Christenheit und Europa*, Munich and Berlin 1931, pp. 18-29.   [2] Above, p. 25.

[3] *De Mon.*, III. xiv. 7: ' . . . non modo Asiani et Affricani omnes, quin etiam maior pars Europam colentium . . . '.

[4] *Comento alla Divina Commedia*, ed. D. Guerri ('Scrittori d'Italia'), iii. 180: 'e cosí come quello che verso Affrica si distende, chiamano Affricano, cosí questo, Europico, il quale si stende infino all' isola di Creti, dovi dicemmo terminarsi il mare Egeo. E cosí l'isola di Creti appare essere in su 'l confine di queste tre parti del mondo.'

[5] *Catholicon*, Lyons 1489, s.v. 'Europa'. Curiously enough the formula 'Historia Europaica' is employed for certain endorsements on degree documents in Edinburgh University. I do not know why this was chosen. It was first used in 1927. On the German *Europaïsch*, see J. P. Krebs, ed. J. H. Schmalz, *Antibarbarus der lateinischen Sprache*, 2 vols., Basle 1905-7, i. 528.

Crete seems to lie on the borders of the three parts of the world'.

In Pius II, however, the word has come to stay. Its usefulness made it have real significance. *Europaeus* is, moreover, the form which was to develop into vernacular forms. Pius therefore may be credited with taking an important step. Europe came of age when 'European' ceased to be merely a dictionary word. Even more important, Pius makes it clear that the word was interchangeable with 'Christian'. 'The events which happened among the Europeans', he writes, 'or those who are called Christians.'[1]

In using Europe and European the pope was also probably influenced by humanist preferences for a classical as against a medieval Latin word. The trend, as is well known, was to substitute where possible a word of undoubtedly authentic classical authority for a word with medieval associations—*templum* for *ecclesia*, *divus* for *sanctus* and so on.[2] Such preferences did not, of course, affect the basic terminology of religion. 'Christian' as such is not capable of paraphrase. But there can be no doubt that humanists were largely responsible for the rapid growth of a preference for *respublica Christiana* instead of *Christianitas*, *terra Christiana*, which had been current alternatives in the medieval period. After all, *Christianitas* was incapable of use in a hexameter line and for the poet was thus almost doomed to extinction. Even writers with no pretensions to humanism on an Italian scale found themselves being driven in this way to use the word Europe, like the Louvain professor who in about 1454 composed a horoscope for the dauphin Louis of France.[3] If *Chris-*

---

[1] 'Historia de Europa', *Opera Omnia*, Basle 1571, p. 387; Vat. Cod. Lat. 405, fo. 249: 'Quae sub Frederico tertio . . . apud Europeos, aut qui nomine Christiano censentur . . . gesta feruntur'. Cf. Fritzemeyer, *op. cit.*, p. 28.

[2] See R. Sabbadini, *Storia del Ciceronianismo* (above, p. 85, n. 2).

[3] Jean de Wesel, quoted by Kervyn de Lettenhove, Chastellain's *Oeuvres* iii. 447n:

Terrae motus erit in multis partibus orbis
Et peregrinorum turbas Europa movebit.

tianitas was difficult from the view-point of poetic diction, it was no less awkward from the point of view of content. No word was more impregnated with all the sentiments and assumptions from which the humanist was trying to move away. An Italian writing Latin in the fifteenth century thus avoided *Christianitas* (for which he normally used *respublica Christiana*) and tended to use the word Europe. We may perhaps suspect that the normal pressure exerted by humanists against the vocabulary of the *medium aevum* was strengthened, in the case of *Europa*, by contact with the Greeks who were so prominent in fifteenth-century cultural and ecclesiastical matters in Italy. There seems no doubt that Greek writers (for obvious reasons) found the use of Europe more natural than their western contemporaries, though they naturally were not able to endow it with the emotional content we have been describing above.[1] However that may be, *Europa* was clearly preferable for neo-Latin writers to *Christianitas*, and given the influence which Italian cultural innovations were to have in succeeding generations, the practice of the humanists in this respect would doubtless have been decisive in the long run. But there is evidence that the same trend was occurring in northern Europe, irrespective of Italian precept.

If we consider, for example, the French historians of the fifteenth century, we find that for Chastellain Christian and Christendom are the words he commonly uses to describe the political nexus with which he is dealing: princes chrestiens, la universelle crestienté, la sainte cristienté.[2] For his younger contemporary Thomas Basin, while Christendom occurs several times in his Latin history,[3] there is a significant adoption of the word Europe

---

[1] See, for the fifteenth century, the selections from Laonikos Chalkokondyles, Chrysoloras and Kananos, in *Europa im XV Jahrhundert von Byzantinern gesehen*, ed. E. v. Ivanka, F. Grabler, G. Stökl, (Graz 1954).

[2] Chastellain's *Oeuvres*, iii. 10, 73, 75, 76, 77, 206. Cf. i. 6 (Prologue) where the Trojan origin of the Franks naturally involves the word Europe.

[3] Ed. C. Samaran, *Historia Caroli VII*, C.H.F.M.A., ii. 66, 219.

in connection with the Turkish advance—and it is clear that the author more or less equates the two concepts:

King Ladislaw was murdered by poison—a terrible blow this for the whole of Christendom, for he was the most powerful of all Christian kings.... There was a chance that ... he might have driven that ravening beast, the emperor of the Turks, out of Greece and out of the territory of Europe.[1]

And when we arrive at Commynes we have, so to speak, rounded a corner. It is not merely that Christendom occurs less frequently in the *Mémoires* than Europe,[2] but that the two notions are interwoven and the newer one is evidently much the more satisfactory. As for their identity, we have Ghent referred to in contiguous passages as the busiest mercantile centre in Europe and as one of the most pleasure-loving areas of Christendom.[3] Further than that Commynes bases his whole right to make judgements on his 'having knowledge of the greater part of Europe',[4] to being ill-informed about the other two parts of the world.[5] For the realistic analysis Commynes was attempting Christian and non-Christian had small relevance, though he paid service to the virtues of religion. What mattered was a ruler's quality and Commynes treated as exactly on a par a prince like Bayezid II, Moslem and enemy though he was, and a Christian hero like Matthias Corvinus.[6] To move from Commynes, alert and European-minded, to Robert Gaguin, tinged as he is with a faint humanist colour, is to go back again to an earlier age. I do not think that even the word Europe is

[1] *Ibid.*, ii. 244: 'Fuit quippe idem rex Lancelotus veneno extinctus: magnum profecto toti Christianitati vulnus inflictum! Nam cum idem juvenis omnium regum Christianorum potentissimus esset ... spes non modica de eo concipi poterat quod ipse ... illam cruentam bestiam, Turcorum imperatorem, de Grecia et tocius Europe finibus ejecisset.'

[2] I have only noticed one *chrestienté*: ed. Calmette, C.H.F.M.A., ii. 208.

[3] *Loc. cit.* and p. 207.

[4] ii. 156: 'car je cuyde avoir veu et cogneu la meilleure part de Europe.'

[5] ii. 210: 'Je n'ay parlé que de Europe, car je ne suys point informé des deux autres pars, Azie et Affrique.'

[6] ii. 335-40. Some of these points are also touched on by Fritzemeyer in his full discussion of Commynes, *op. cit.*, pp. 28-32.

to be met with in the *Compendium super Francorum gestis*. But I am certain the spirit behind the word is absent; the *Compendium* is a reflection of an older world by a conservative religious with literary ambitions.[1] Valuable as Italian experience and Italian terminology was to be, a consciousness of Europe was growing independently.[2]

A further reflection of this trend and a further influence upon it may be seen in the new cartography of the later middle ages. *Mappaemundi* continued to be made in illustration of the well-known books, Isidore, Macrobius and the rest.[3] But a new and completely different type of map makes its appearance—a map designed to be used not by scholars in a study, but by travellers, above all by mariners. The new maps are called *portolani*.[4]

The earliest surviving example of the new type of map dates from about 1300, but there is evidence of the use of mariners' charts of this kind from the thirteenth century; in any case, such charts cannot have evolved to their early fourteenth century complexity without decades, perhaps centuries, of gradual development.[5] From the viewpoint of technical cartography and scientific geography the *portolani* are a tremendous step forward towards recognizably modern maps. They clearly owed their novel precision to the more accurate navigation which went with the use of the compass. Each portolan was covered by a number of loxodromes, rhumb-lines or 'wind roses', which provided the mariner with the parallels he should use in each day's run.[6] From our point of view the new maps are of significance partly because they provided a

---

[1] See the unpublished doctoral thesis (Edinburgh, 1954) on Gaguin and Aemilius by Miss Katharine Davies.

[2] See further below, p. 99.   [3] Above, p. 53.

[4] The standard work is K. Kretschmer, *Die Italienischen Portolane des Mittelalters*, Berlin 1909; they are also discussed by Beazley (above, p. 37) iii. 572-28. There is a good collection of reproductions in A. E. Nordenskiöld, *Periplus*, Stockholm 1897.

[5] On both points see Beazley, iii. 512-13, Kimble, *Geog. In Mid. Ages*, pp. 190, 225-7; cf. above, p. 6.

[6] The use of the *portolani* in navigation is explained by Kimble, pp. 192-3.

picture of the earth more in conformity with reality than any previous maps; partly because they were largely confined to Europe; and partly because they reflected an interest in the political scene markedly absent in earlier maps.

The scope of the earliest portolan was presumably Mediterranean. But the *Carte Pisane* of 1300 or thereabouts already embraces, somewhat scantily, the Atlantic coast of Europe.[1] The 'Carignano' map of 1300-5 is thus described:

> The Black Sea is represented in its entirety, with a general contour little inferior to that of the Mediterranean; the South and West of Britain, from about the Isle of Wight to the Mull of Cantyre, together with the East Irish coast, are of surprising excellence; while the ocean shore of Europe, from Cadiz to Calais, appears with a comparative accuracy equally meritorious, though less unexpected. The projection of Denmark, again, though crowded up too close upon England and the Channel, is well conceived; Scandinavia, though clearly outside the horizon of detailed knowledge, is shown as a peninsula, for the first time in existing cartography; and the Azov Sea, even if somewhat exaggerated upon its Western side, is pretty well realized upon its Eastern.[2]

Later in the century the great Catalan Atlas of 1375 and the Majorcan charts of the 1380s represent an even further development, in which not only is Europe better depicted, but new knowledge about Asia and Africa is included.[3] There was to be a steady multiplication of such works, and the scientific handling of the new cartography, together with the rediscovery of Ptolemy's work, precipitated the study of projections and the construction of globe-maps. In this connection we should note what have been called 'the earliest separate maps of the three continents'.[4] Probably made about 1350 in Constantinople by Nikephorus Gregoras as part of a Greek Ptolemy now at Milan, these maps clearly owe a good deal to the portolan tradition.

In the fourteenth and fifteenth centuries it was thus

[1] Beazley, iii. plate facing p. 518.   [2] Beazley, iii. 519.   [3] *Ibid.*, 525-7.
[4] Konrad Miller, *Die ältesten Separatkarten der 3 Erdteile*, Stuttgart 1931.

possible to look at maps which represented the surface of
the earth with a fair degree of accuracy. It is significant
that many people did consult the new maps who were
not travellers. This may be inferred from several con-
siderations. First of all the surviving examples of the
portolani and similar maps are nearly all beautifully constructed and well preserved. Clearly the working copies
of sailors seldom survived to be collected by amateurs of
geographical knowledge; but such amateurs went out of
their way to obtain copies specially for reference.[1]
Secondly, purely literary works were occasionally illustrated with maps based, not upon the old conventional
pictures of an earlier day, but upon the fresh and accurate
charts now available. Examples of such illustrations are
the maps in the crusading treatise of Marino Sanudo, the
Liber secretorum Fidelium Crucis (completed in 1321) and
those in the Italian poem on cosmography, *La Sfera* of
Leonardo Dati (f. 1425). Above all it can be shown with
a fair degree of certainty that Dante consulted maps of
the portolan type. This is the most plausible explanation
of his occasionally remarkable statements of spatial re-
lationships—such as that Marseilles was opposite the
North African port of Bugia.[2] Even more revealing is
his description of the birthplace of St. Dominic at
Calahorra:

Towards that part where sweet Zephyr riseth to open the new
leaves, wherewith Europe seeth herself reclad, not far off from the
smiting of the waves, behind which, because of their long stretch,
the sun sometimes hideth himself from all, the fortune-favoured
Calahorra sitteth under the protection of the mighty shield, whereon
submits the lion, and subdueth.[3]

This passage identifies the place by saying that it is near
the west coast of Europe, and that it is in Castile, whose

[1] Beazley, iii. 520-1 and plate; Atiya, *Crusade in Later Middle Ages*, pp.
116-24.
[2] *Par.*, ix. 88-93.
[3] Trans. P. H. Wicksteed, *Par.*, xii. 46-54:
    In quella parte, ove surge ad aprire
        Zefiro dolce le novelle fronde,
        di che si vede Europa rivestire,   [*contd. opposite*

arms 'bear a castle in the first and third quarters, and a lion in the second and fourth'. It is likely that Dante got not only his Zephyr from looking at a map, but also his coat of arms.[1]

For, besides depicting a truer outline of the continents, many of the *portolani* carried symbolical indications of the political authority in each area. These indications were small flags or shields with the coat of arms, or what purported to be a coat of arms, of the principality or town. These are found in the 'Carignano' portolan (1300-5), and in other later examples, some of which may be consulted in published collections.[2] This armorial preoccupation also distinguishes a curious fourteenth-century work, the so-called *Book of the Knowledge of all the Kingdoms, Lands and Lordships that are in the World*[3] which 'is the very earliest representation of the flags of all nations'.[4] The Spanish friar who compiled it almost certainly made use of a portolano chart, such as the Carignano, with shields. A further development is the map made in Constance by Andrew Walsperger in 1448. This shows Christian cities marked by red dots and infidel cities by black dots.[5]

> non molto lungi al percuoter de l'onde,
> dietro a quali, per la lunga foga
> lo sol tal volta ad ogni uom si nasconde,
> siede la fortunata Calaroga
> sotto la protezion del grande scudo,
> in che soggiace il leone e soggioga.

[1] On Dante's use of maps cf. Assunto Mori, 'La geografia di Dante', *Archivio di Storia della Scienza*, Rome 1922, iii. 57-69, esp. pp. 61, 65 and n. 15; and R. Salomon, *Opicinus de Canistris, Weltbild und Bekentnisse eines Avignonischen Kleriker des 14 Jahrhunderts*, 2 vols., London 1936, p. 60. I have not seen Magnaghi, 'Il quarnero dantesco', *Geografia*, 3-4, 1921; nor the article (perhaps never published) by G. Boffito on 'Cartografia dantesca' referred to in *Giornale Dantesco*, xxiv. 103n.

[2] Beazley, iii. 475, 519 has sections of 'Carignano' and so has Nordenskiöld, *Periplus*, plate V. For later examples of heraldic maps see Nordenskiöld, plate VIII (Angelino Dulcert, 1339), XXII (Conte Freducci, 1497), XXV (Georgio Calapoda, 1552), XXIX (Domingo Olives, 1568). Cf. Beazley, iii. 429, Kimble, pl. viii (Catalan Atlas of 1375).

[3] Hakluyt Society, 2nd series, xxix (1912), ed. Sir Clements Markham.

[4] *Ibid.*, p. xii.

[5] K. Kretschmer, 'Eine neue mittelalterliche Weltkarte der Vatikanischen Bibliothek', *Zeitschrift der Gesellschaft für Erdkunde zu Berlin*, xxvi (1891), 371-406 and plate 10; see p. 377 for Walsperger's explanation of his symbols. No infidel city is shown in Spain.

Now, however fanciful some of these heraldic symbols may be, in one important respect they were revealing: as plotted on a map the areas of Moslem domination were marked by the Crescent of Islam (see plate II).[1]

Roger Bacon had already pointed out how essential it was to plot the disposition of religions, how hazardous not to know 'when one enters Christian territory, and when the territory of schismatics, Saracens, Tartars', and so on.[2] The maker of the new maps, at all events when he was designing for a cultivated amateur, made it clear where Christendom began and ended. This was probably even less a matter of indifference to sailors and travellers who might otherwise sail unwittingly into captivity, ransom or worse in the fourteenth century than it had been two generations earlier. In some ways the new maps were less continent-conscious than the old literary diagrams designed to show a symmetrical world pivoted on Jerusalem, pointing a moral in an erudite manuscript or (as at Ebsdorf or Hereford) on the wall of a church. Such diagrams positively insisted on the tripartite globe and invoked the memory of Japheth, Shem and Ham. But if the new maps were untidy and (by literary standards) uninformative, they not only corresponded with the new realities of travel, commerce and science as practical men found them in the fourteenth century, but they often revealed more sharply than ever before the virtual identity of Christendom and Europe. The first maps to do this were, therefore, drawn when Christendom as an active principle was in decline. The *mappaemundi* never distinguished between Christian Europe, Moslem Africa and

---

[1] The illustration shows a portion of a portolan of 1497 made by a member of the Ancona family of Freducci (Nordenskiöld, plate XXII, cf. his text p. 64a). This late example was chosen because it lent itself to small scale reproduction. The area depicted includes the west end of the Mediterranean and the adjacent Atlantic coasts of Spain and Africa.

[2] 'Receperunt etiam pericula infinita, eo quod nesciverunt quando intraverunt regiones fidelium, quando schismatorum, quando Saracenorum, quando Tartarorum. . . . Quamplurimi enim a negotiis Christianorum maximis sunt frustrati eo quod regionum distinctiones nesciverunt', *Opus Majus*. ed, Bridges, i. 301.

Asia. This was revealed by many of the *portolani*.[1] It is probably because of the new awareness revealed most clearly in the *portolani* that we find two late examples of conventional maps which may indicate some desire to distinguish the continents. One is from a fourteenth-century manuscript: its simple T-O pattern is diversified by Europe being coloured differently from Asia and Africa.[2] The other is in a fifteenth-century manuscript and shows a drawing in each of the portions of the tri-partite world. There is little to choose between the senti-ments expressed by Asia and Europe: both are represented by town buildings. But Africa is shown as a jungle with wild animals.[3] If this was the most that conventional cartography could do to accommodate the new spirit it was clearly not worthy to survive.

The fifteenth century thus saw alongside the traditional picture, which continued to be represented for long enough,[4] the emergence in the new maps of a visual apprehension of the world in fresh terms. The old Chris-tendom was in practice confined to Europe. 'Europe now alone is Christian.' Given this, given a universal church that was universal no longer—in Europe, let alone over a wider area—and which was struggling ineffectively to protect European Christendom from outside attack, given a disinclination in certain circles to use the very word 'Christendom', and the stage was set for the gradual emergence of a notion of Europe which would slowly evict Christendom from its hardly won place as an inte-grating notion. Europe was to be a less ambitious project than Christendom, but hardly less influential.

[1] Appropriately enough, Mohammed II the Conqueror was said to possess 'a map showing the realms and provinces of Europe'. P. Wittek, in *The Fall of Constantinople: a symposium*, School of Oriental and African Studies, London University, 1955, p. 40.   [2] Santarem, *Essai*, iii, §§ 71-2, 73, 67.
[3] College of Heralds, Arundel MS. 53, fo. 3v.
[4] A humanist environment alone was not sufficient to oust the cartography of an earlier day. See the medals of Francesco Laurana (d. about 1502) and Sperando of Mantua (d. after 1504), both of which have the older kind of map on them: G. F. Hill, *Corpus of the Italian Medals of the Renaissance*, London, i. 95, ii. plate 16, no. 63.

CHAPTER 6

RENAISSANCE CHRISTENDOM

WE have seen the old notion of Christendom weakened by internal contradiction and pressure from without. We have seen in the fourteenth century, and even more in the fifteenth, a European self-consciousness emerging. Yet it was long before Europe gained an outright victory, before Christendom was driven into the limbo of the archaic and the precious. Pius II, who provided important illustrations of the trend towards a European spirit, used the phrase *Respublica Christiana* frequently in his writings—more frequently (it may confidently be stated) than he used the word Europe. And if by Christendom he meant Europe, that was precisely the ambiguity which was to persist. From 1400 to 1700, and in certain areas and contexts perhaps beyond this terminus, the new unity was confounded with the old, as was not unnatural in a European society in which religion was still an active constituent of public and private life. If the sixteenth and seventeenth centuries witnessed further developments inimical to the reality of Christendom and contributing, more or less directly, to the reality of Europe, the viability of Christendom is all the more impressive.

Of these developments we may consider first the continued loss of centralized organization in the Church. As explained above, the church entered the fifteenth century in a provincialized state. The old universal orders tended to be grouped within national frontiers, the *legatus natus* acted as a symbol of the same process which led princes to keep resident ambassadors at the papal court. The pope was a prince, yet one whose powers trespassed theoretically on the preserves of a galaxy of other sovereigns, jealous of their independence, anxious to master still further the relics of autonomy in their clerical subjects. The devout still urged reform but they saw it in terms of a conciliar movement, unaware of the papal conjuring trick which had vaporized the decree *Frequens* of the Council of Constance. Princes, too, paid lip service to the council, for it would have strengthened a federal church and for the same reason it was resisted by popes, who could not be certain that a future council would not attempt, as Constance had done legally and Basle illegally, to dethrone and shackle the bishop of Rome.

The Lutheran crisis falls into place in this situation. Explosive it certainly was—but not because of the reformer's programme so much as because his actions commanded lay support on a hitherto unprecedented scale. For Germans the destruction of Luther would have meant not merely a stronger pope, but a stronger emperor, the curtailment of princely independence. Coupled with that went a social upheaval which gave a degree of popular support to 'reform' that it had lacked, for instance, in Wycliffe's England. For all his force of personality and for all the undoubted power he exerted, Luther was no more than the spark which ignited a very combustible mass. After all, in England a break occurred with the papacy of a totally uncompromising nature, which owed next to nothing to doctrinal differences. Henry VIII's orthodoxy faltered only on the very point under discussion: the headship of the church. Had the pope been able to exercise the habitually pliant diplomacy of his office he would have temporized and avoided a break, but only at the cost of surrendering further to the pretensions of monarchy. As it was Henry did his best to avoid being compromised with reforming tendencies, and Anglicanism (as well as large scale dissent from Anglicanism) came later. There was not much difference, except at the apex, between Henry VIII's *Ecclesia Anglicana* and Edward III's.

Just as England illuminates the continental reformation by showing its roots in princely autocracy and popular resentment of 'Rome', so Scotland reveals another aspect of the reformation: the action of protestant princes in resisting the pope enormously increased the power of catholic princes over the churches in their territories. The diplomatic pressure exerted at the papal court by James V of Scotland was effective out of all proportion to the standing of his small, poor and divided country. Again and again in his demands upon the pope for privileges and graces the same argument is rehearsed: 'unless you do this for me, I shall not be able to retain the loyalty of my people to the Roman Church; with Lutheranism in Germany and disobedience in England, my people must see the tangible fruits of their Roman allegiance'. To these representations popes could offer no resistance and the Scottish church, stripped of its wealth (which went to the Scottish nobility) was nullified and made ineffective by a series of papal bulls. Elsewhere, as in Spain, France and Catholic Germany, similar appeals made power over the disposal of church property the test of obedience to Rome. Luther and the protestant princes benefited their Catholic enemies as much as they benefited themselves.

That protestants continued often to think in terms of Christendom, we shall see in a moment. Important as that is, the significance of the reformation and the counter reformation lies in their finally putting churches in the hands of governments, thus accomplishing a trend which had been in progress for centuries. Europe after the sixteenth century may have gradually abandoned confessional wars, but only at the price of agreeing to differ as to what in fact Christianity entailed. When this occurred a long step had been taken to making 'Christian' a vague cultural concept and Christendom a theory of the past.

The overseas expansion of the late fifteenth and later centuries was another factor influencing the notion of Europe. This was not because the discovery of a new continent in America shattered at a blow traditional geography, and especially the traditional geography of religion. If it seemed unlikely that a descendant of Noah could have peopled America as part of the historical process so familiar to Christendom, it was not until the eighteenth century that it was finally shown that the Americas were physically cut off from the land mass of Europe and Asia and even then it was easier to account for the population of the New World than for that in the Antipodes.

Where the greatly increased knowledge of the world did act as an immediate stimulus was by provoking a wider public interest than before in the differences between Europeans and the peoples of other continents. In this the dispersion of knowledge of the Orient was for long more important than that of America, where the primitive natives of the north had little that was culturally significant to offer their conquerors and where the more advanced civilizations of the centre were destroyed in the act of conquest. It has, in fact, been shown that during the sixteenth century books in French on the New World were relatively few in comparison with those on Asia Minor and the Orient and that—contrary to what one might have supposed—the proportion of them drops as the century progresses.[1]

The activity of students of geography in the Renaissance period was particularly notable in northern Europe.[2] We find the repeated publication of works of ancient geography, frequently with descriptive matter included, as in the successive editions of Ptolemy by Waldseemüller

---

[1] G. Atkinson, *Les nouveaux horizons de la Renaissance française*, Paris 1935, pp. 10-12, 29.

[2] Atkinson, *op. cit.*; S. Gunther, 'Die Humanismus in seinem Einfluss auf die Entwicklung der Erdkunde', *Geog. Zeitschrift*, vi (1900), 65-89; E. G. R. Taylor, *Tudor Geography*, 1930.

(1513), Fries (1522), Pirckheimer (1525), Servetus (1535) and others. Italian humanist geographical works were also esteemed, particularly the writings of Aeneas Sylvius, whose *Descriptio Asiae et Europae* was separately reprinted six times. Other evidence is provided by the constant composition of new works on general geography, from Peter Apianus's *Cosmographia* (1524 and frequent reprints)[1] and Joachim Vadianus's *Epitome trium terrae partim* (Zurich 1534) down to the more elaborate books of the second half of the sixteenth century, such as the *Habitus praecipuorum populorum* (H. Weigel, Nürnberg 1577) and J.-J. Boissard's *Habitus variorum gentium* (Metz 1581).[2] Even more significant perhaps, and certainly much better known, was the production of sixteenth-century cartography. Waldseemüller's *Carta Itineraria Europae* appeared in 1511; from then on the number of continental maps grows in number and improves in quality, the most important moment in this development being Mercator's *Atlas* of 1595.[3] Based on Ptolemy, on the empirical construction of globes and on the rapidly developing understanding of the problems of surveying, the cartography of the sixteenth century provided contemporaries with a surer picture of the world and its parts than any previously available.

Educated contemporaries were, in fact, quick to respond to the quickening sense of a world in which continents were important, though the older cosmography lost ground only slowly among the less cultivated.[4] It is, as one would anticipate, common among Latin writers to find Europa occurring frequently: this merely continued a trend already noticed.[5] As random examples we may cite Platina's reference to Pope Nicholas V sending

[1] Including important ones by Gemma Phrysius.
[2] See below, p. 104.
[3] The map of Europe had appeared earlier, in 1572.
[4] Cf. L. Olschki, *op. cit.*
[5] Above, p. 87.

EVROPA.

Sceptrum Europa gerit, pars præstantissima mundi
Lætaq; fert vinum munus Iacche tuum.

40.

PLATE IV. 'Europa', from Ph. Galle, *Prosopographia*, 1579. See p. 104.

scholars 'throughout Europe',[1] and two other Italian historians, Paulus Aemilius in France talking of France's former hegemony in Europe[2] and Polydore Vergil in England describing the Franco-Scottish alliance as the longest established and firmest treaty in Europe.[3] The use was, of course, by no means restricted to Italians. Erasmus uses the word frequently[4]; Conrad Celtis provides a good example for Germany, Robert Estienne for France,[5] and John Major for Scotland.[6] For reasons already indicated[7] the word had a special appeal for versifiers.[8]

More significant is the continued trend in vernacular usage. The passage of time sees an ever increasing tendency to use the word Europe. For instance the French pamphlet, *Le débat des héraulx d'armes*, composed about 1450 as part of French propaganda against England, does not use the word Europe, though the word Chrétienté is several times found. Yet when the English *Debate* was adapted from this (1550) to form an anti-French tract, there is no mention of Christendom, but there is a mention of Europe.[9] For Clément Marot the word has not much use, though it is occasionally found in his poems; but it is Chrétiens and Chrétienté that really move him.[10] For Ronsard in the next generation the whole notion of the continents is

---

[1] *Vitae pontificum*, ed. Gaida, RR.II.SS, p. 338: 'Misit et litteratos viros per omnem Europam.'

[2] Bibliothèque Nationale, MS. Lat. 5935 f. 1: 'Francia illa cuius imperium Europae ferme universae augustum sanctumque—nuper erat'; again Lat. 5936, f. 17v.

[3] *Anglica Historia*, ed. 1555, p. 681: '. . . cum tota Europa non alia diuturnior sanctiorque reperiatur'; cf. *De inventoribus rerum*, Elzevir 1671, p. 177.

[4] Cf. below.

[5] C. Celtis, *Selections*, ed. L. Forster, Cambridge 1948, p. 42: 'terram nostram maximam Europae partem'. R. Estienne: 'Lutetia, Galliae urbs maxima . . . magnitudine et frequentia certat cum maximis Europae urbibus', cit. Elizabeth Armstrong, *Robert Estienne*, Cambridge 1954, p. 90.

[6] *Historia majoris Britannicae*, Edinburgh 1740, p. 15: 'Ex omni Europae regione illic [London] mercatorum naves invenies.'

[7] Above, p. 88.

[8] E.g. Marullus,*Carmina*, ed. A. Perosa, Zurich 1951, p. 211, and the student poem quoted by H. de Vocht, *History of the Collegium Trilingue Lovaniense*, iii (1954), p. 120 n. 4.

[9] Ed. L. Pannier and P. Meyer, S.A.T.F., Paris 1877, pp. 16, 27, 37, 39, 103.

[10] *Oeuvres*, ed. P. Jannet, ii. 105, 110-1, 112 etc.

H

filled with rhetorical splendour:

> L'Europe est trop petite, et l'Asie et l'Afrique
> Pour toy qui te verras de tout le monde Roy;
> Aussi le Ciel n'aguere a fait naistre pour toy
> Du Milieu de la mer la nouvelle Amérique.[1]

That this is far from being solely poetical and dramatic we can see from the pages of Etienne Pasquier's *Recherches de la France*, where Europe is a frequently encountered word. Here, for example, is an instance in which the antiquary invokes for Charlemagne some of the magic Ronsard had bestowed on Henri III: 'Ainsi receut Charlemagne la Couronne de l'Empire, et fut sacré Empereur par les mains du grand Pontife de Rome avecques un applaudissement general de toute l'Europe.'[2]

The literary use of the continents steadily multiplied. 'I have seen a play', Cervantes makes one of his characters say in *Don Quixote*, 'whose first act opened in Europe, its second in Asia and its third in Africa. And if there had been four acts, the fourth no doubt would have finished up in America; and so it would have been played in all four quarters of the globe.'[3] This observation was prompted by a criticism of the unrealities of the theatre. A growing concern for the dramatic unities was to stifle such eccentricities, but the poets were under no such ban.

> The Westerne treasure, Easterne spicerie,
> Europe, and Afrique, and the unknown rest[4]

form one of the glittering threads running through seventeenth-century verse. The ability to extend the vision of 'the hemisphere of earth' so that it embraced not only the narrow world of Christendom but the vastly enlarged horizons of the contemporary world irresistibly appealed to the poets.[5]

---

[1] Ed. G. Cohen, N.R.F., i. 299; cf. 307, 483, 936; ii. 153.
[2] *Recherches*, Paris 1633, p. 163C.
[3] *Don Quixote*, i. ch. 48 (ed. Penguin, p. 429).
[4] J. Donne, 'The second Anniversary', 228-9, Oxford edn., p. 233. For other instances of continental imagery in Donne cf. *ibid.*, pp. 35, 107, 336-7.
[5] Cf. Adam's vision in *Paradise Lost*, xi. 385-411.

The artists took a hand in this development. The older themes germane to our enquiry were not neglected: Noah and his three sons were frequently depicted by painters and engravers. But this tradition, which as noted above,[1] had been associated with the continents in the middle ages, did not acquire any such association in the Renaissance. Noah drunk, the cursing of Ham and his progeny, the blessed inheritance of Japheth and Shem, are moralized, but not in any sense which could contribute much to an awareness of the superiority of Europe.[2] Europa, however, had a more promising career.

The rape of Europa had survived in medieval iconography, but in a manner devoid of life. As with other classical themes, the Renaissance clothed the picture of Europa in a more faithful framework of classical *motifs* and imparted to it a 'joyful sensuality'.[3] The reproduction of illustrations in editions of Ovid[4] and the *Hypnerotomachia Poliphili* of Francesco Colonna diffused this invigorated tradition, which produced many fine works of art: Dürer's drawing in the Albertina and the paintings by Titian and Veronese are signal examples; and there are many other minor Renaissance examples of the same theme.[5] These changes, in themselves, did not contribute to the enrichment of a continental awareness, however.

This resulted rather from developments at an artistically

[1] Above, p. 53.

[2] D. C. Allen, *Legend of Noah*, pp. 168-73, discusses most of the important paintings and engravings. To his references may be added the fine engraving in H. Schedel's *Liber Chronicarum*, Nuremberg 1493, in which Japheth's especial virtue is perhaps indicated by his standing apart, eyes covered, while Shem covers his father's nakedness (see plate III); and the Bellini painting at Besançon. It may also be significant that in the fifteenth-century *Mistère du viel Testament* (S.A.T.F. 1878), i. 240-52, the lead in reproving Ham is taken by Japheth.

[3] See E. Panofsky's letter in *Art Bulletin*, xxx (1948), 242a; and his *Studies in Iconology*, pp. 29-30.

[4] M. D. Henkel, 'Illustrierte Ausgaben von Ovids Metamorphosen im xv-xvii Jahrhundts', *Bibl. Warburg*, vi (1926-7), 57-144.

[5] For instance the painting by Liberale da Verona in the Louvre; a bas-relief from the Hôtel d'Escoville (1533-41) at Caen, illustrated in R. Schneider, 'Notes sur l'influence artistique du Songe de Poliphile', *Etudes Italiennes*, ii (1920), 1-16, 65-73, figs. 9 and 10; the relief on Clare Bridge, Cambridge (to which my attention was directed by Mr Giles Robertson).

less august and more vulgar level. On the one hand the rapidly multiplying books of geographical description which are found in the late sixteenth and early seventeenth centuries frequently embellish title pages with personified continents; on the other there were political interests which prompted artists in the same direction. Of this second influence little need be said, for it was apparently not particularly important: the younger Frans Franken's allegory of the four continents presenting gifts to Charles V is the best example[1]—a kind of pictorial parallel to the verses of Ronsard quoted above. More important are the descriptive geographical works: *Habitus praecipuorum populorum* (Nürnberg 1577); Ph. Galle's *Prosopographia* (1579), Ripa's *Iconologia* (1611), and others. In the title pages and illustrations of these works[2] we find the continents associated with ideas: Europa—crowned, cuirassed, holding a sceptre and orb, with weapons, scientific instruments, a palette, books and Christian symbols; Asia—garlanded and richly dressed, holding an incense-burner, and supported by camels and monkeys; Africa—naked, with elephants and lions, snakes and palms, and often with the sun's rays like a halo on the head; America—naked, with a feathered head-dress, holding a bow and arrow. Of the separate illustrations in such works the engraving by Ph. Galle (Plate IV) is one of the earliest and one of the best. In these ways Europe in its own right, besides Europa by reason of her rape, entered the canon of European art, occasionally thereafter attracting the attention of a great artist—as in the Rubens 'Four Quarters of the World' at Vienna.[3]

The artists were thus displaying a growing awareness

[1] Amsterdam, Rijksmuseum 935.

[2] Cf. also the drawings by Martin de Vos, Print Room, Plantin Museum, Antwerp; R. van Marle, *Iconographie de l'art prophane: Allegories et Symboles* ii. 309-10; B. Knipping, *De iconografie van de contra-reformatie in de Nederlanden* Hilversum 1940, pp. 158-65; James H. Hyde, 'L'iconographie des quatre parties du monde dans les tapisseries', *Gazette des Beaux Arts* (1924), ii. 253-72.

[3] Kunsthistorisches Museum.

of qualitative differences between Europe and the other continents. Among writers the beginnings of this are much older. Traces of such distinctions are to be found, as we have seen,[1] in some writings of antiquity and these naturally attracted the attention of humanists. Presumably it was in this way that Aeneas Sylvius was led to remark in his *Germania* that 'the inhabitants of Asia are always considered inferior to the inhabitants of Europe'[2]; and perhaps Machiavelli stressed the superiority of the European political system in part because of ancient examples.[3] But greater knowledge filled out this tradition. The explorers could hardly fail to be impressed (for example) by the attitude to gold in the New World, where it was 'esteemed as nought', so Amerigo Vespucci reported.[4] From then onwards the mariners and cosmographers accumulated a mass of detailed differences which added to the more obvious religious distinction in cutting off the Far East and the New World from Europe. Camoens, writing his *Lusiads* in the 1550s and 1560s, calls Europe 'the home of strong and warlike peoples' and stresses its fertility:— 'Proud Europe', 'Christian Europe' 'is more advanced and more renowned in its governance than the others'.[5] When we find Peter Apianus comparing Europe favourably with Asia and Africa, though it is less in extent, we can take it that he is going on what seemed to him concrete evidence.[6] Later writers were, as we shall see, to take this a great deal further,[7] but a symbol of the position achieved by the middle of the sixteenth century is the *Cosmographia Universalis* of the Protestant Hebraist, Sebastian Münster. This book appeared first at Basle in

---

[1] Above, pp. 32, 38. [2] *Germania*, ed. Paparelli, Florence 1949, p. 104.
[3] See below, p. 122.
[4] 'Quatuor Americi Vespuci navigationes', in *Cosmographie Introductio* (Grüniger, Strasbourg, 1509), sig. E. i: 'Aurum uniones jocalia caeteraque similia quae in hac Europa pro divitiis habemus, nihil estimant.'
[5] *Lusiads*, trs. W. C. Atkinson, 1952, pp. 49, 141, 161-4, 236.
[6] *Cosmographia*, Paris 1551, f. 30v: 'Populorum gentiumque virtute longe Asia et Africa praestantior: caeteris tamen terrae partibus minor.'
[7] Atkinson, *Nouveaux horizons, passim*; and below, p. 119 ff.

German in 1544[1] and passed through a number of versions
in other vernaculars and in Latin. 'Europe,' he writes,
'though smaller than the other parts of the world, is the
most populous, fertile and cultivated.... For in Europe
one does not find the huge solitudes, sterile deserts and
cruel heat of Africa. However remote the locality in
Europe in it men have built habitations.... And so
Europe is self-sufficient in both peace and war. It has
men enough to fight, to till the fields and to dwell in
towns.'[2] 'Europa sufficientissima sibi': what nonsense this
would have seemed to Gregory VII or Innocent III.

In view of the preceding evidence of interest in the term
Europe it is not surprising that the adjective European
makes a rapid advance in the sixteenth century. The first
use of it was, it will be recalled, in a humanist context[3]
and at first sixteenth-century instances seem to occur, as
one would suppose, in Latin works. The title of a work
by a Polish annalist, Matthias à Michow, seems the earliest
sixteenth-century instance: De Sarmatica Asiatica et Euro-
paea, 1518.[4] Next comes Erasmus's treatise, Consultatio de
bello Turcis inferendo, which first appeared, in the form of
a letter to J. Rinck, in 1530.[5] Here the word Europe is
naturally common enough[6] but more notable is the phrase
'European wealth' which we find.[7] Many more instances
must lie buried in the largely unknown Latin literature of
the Renaissance. In any event, by the second half of the
sixteenth century we find the adjective in some of the

[1] All. Deutsche Biog., xxiii. 31, says 1543.

[2] Op. cit., ed. Basle 1559, pp. 40-1: 'Est itaque Europa regio reliquis orbis
partibus minor, sed populosissima, fertilissima atque cultissima.... Nam in
Europa non inveniuntur tam vastae solitudines, tam steriles arenae, et tam
ingens calor omnia exurens quam in Africa. Nullus est locus aut regio in
Europa abiecta, in qua homines sibi non fecerint mansiones.... Est ergo
Europa ad pacem et ad bellum sufficientissima sibi. Nam habet abunde
multitudinem pugnacem, et quae agros colat, et quae urbes contineat quoque.'

[3] Above, p. 86.

[4] Taylor, Tudor Geography, p. 224; Abel Mansuy, Le monde slave et les
classiques français au XVI–XVII siècles, Paris 1912, p. 12, gives some details.

[5] Op. Ep., ed. Allen, viii. 382 (no. 2285, 17 March 1530).

[6] Consultatio, ed. J. Maire, Leyden 1643, pp. 22, 30, etc.

[7] Ibid., p. 22: 'Europaeas opes'.

vernaculars. One would expect Italian to be first in the field. Certainly the occurrence of the word in a text printed in Ramusio's *Viaggi* in 1559 can hardly be the first, though it is the earliest I have noted.[1] With French and English we are on somewhat safer ground. Godefroy quotes the phrase 'Quelque lengue europienne que ce soit' from Bonnivard's *Advis et devis des lengues* of 1563. The earliest English usage so far noted dates from 1593 and is found in John Eliot, *Ortho-Epia Gallica* ('O pearle of rich European bounds').[2] It may well be the case that earlier instances will be noticed. It is sufficient here to observe that by the start of the seventeenth century the literatures of the main European countries had acquired a word which was to be much in demand.

Within the framework of an environment slowly becoming more *European*, older ideas continued to develop. Noah and his progeny were still relevant to speculation as they were to imaginative writing. In the *Boke of St. Albans* (1486) we find some discussion of Japheth and Shem, who were both gentlemen as opposed to Ham, who was cursed and was a churl.[3] More attention was, however, given to Ham than to his brothers: Lemaire de Belges explained that Ham, by his magic arts, made Noah impotent and that this was the reason why he was cursed[4]; and a legend that the cause of Noah's wrath was really the incontinence (and worse) of Ham in the Ark itself began a career which was to blacken still further his memory.[5] The theologians, both Catholic and Protestant, continued of course to comment on the Genesis story

---

[1] Taylor, p. 214. Presumably the translation of the Polish work referred to above.

[2] Mr. J. C. Maxwell drew my attention to this; it is quoted by P. Ure in his edition of Shakespeare's *Richard II*, 1956, p. 206. The *New English Dictionary*'s earliest example is from Knole's *History of the Turks*, 1603.

[3] Ed. by W. Blades, 1881, sig. a i - a iiv. This is the same notion as that referred to above, p. 41.

[4] *Antiquitez des Gaules et Singularitez de Troye*, ed. A. J. Stecher, 1882-91, i. 25.

[5] For the scabrous details see P. Bayle, *Dictionnaire*, s.v. 'Cham'.

which was for long unquestioned as a description of the peopling of the earth.[1] So, too, did those historians who dealt with the earliest periods. Sir Walter Raleigh's *History of the World* contained a map in which the descendants of Noah are depicted, moving like columns of ants, from the Tower of Babel.[2] It remained possible, though perhaps after about 1600 a little precious, to refer to the continents merely by reference to the sons of Noah: 'whether where Japhet dwelt, or Cham, or Sem'.[3]

The Trojan story was also lively enough, at all events in the early days of the sixteenth century, mainly as a result of the forgery of Annius of Viterbo, who in 1498 published at Rome what purported to be the lost texts of Berosus and Manetho which filled in the gaps of Gaulish history. A little later John Trithemius, abbot of Sponheim, a more reputable figure than Annius, composed an imaginative history of the Franks and 'discovered' the chronicle of Hunebald. With this material it was possible to elaborate the Trojan origin of every European people, to account for the dispersion of the arts and sciences, and to provide an etymology of illustrious antiquity for every place name. This work was accomplished by many writers, of whom the most famous was Jean Lemaire de Belges, in his *Illustrations de Gaule et Singularitez de Troye*.[4] National pride was the spirit which encouraged this remarkable wave of legend; it was the conflict of national claims which produced critics. The Italians, for example, bitterly resented the Frankish myth as advanced by Lemaire de Belges, and patriotism thus provided a motive for the destruction of Annius's deceit or credulity—which (to do Italians justice) had provoked suspicion at once among a few scholars as well as admiration from others.[5]

---

[1] See D. C. Allen's study, quoted above, p. 53, n. 1.

[2] Edition of 1634, pp. 152-3.

[3] Donne, *ed. cit.*, p. 337.

[4] On these developments see Joly (cited above, p. 49, n. 5), pp. 541-98.

[5] Joly, pp. 599-600; Tiraboschi, *Storia della letteratura italiana*, Florence 1809, vi (pt. 2), p. 652.

90

80

Indigene universæ Americæ Christum ignorant atqʒ Diabolum colunt, niſi quibuſdam in locis, quo Hiſpani colonias ſuas deduxerunt, quarum præcipuas hoc + ſigno notavimus.

70

60

Nova Francia

Groenland

AMERICA SEPTEN

Hybernia

Canadenses

Terra nova

50

Galli

TRION.

PA

Hispa:

40

nia

Florida

Barbaria

Cuba Hiſpaniola

MAR DEL

A

Bile

F

30

NORT

Tombutto

Panama

GUINE

Caribana

+ AMERICA ME

Aethio

Peru

Brasilia

Pernibuco

via

picus

20

RIDIONALIS

Oceant

Chili

10

MAR

Patagonum

290 300   310   Regio 330   340   350   360   10   20   30

DELZUR

50

60

Tierra del Fogo

DESIGNATIO ORBIS
CHRISTIANI

PLATE V. Map of World religions by J

From *Purchas his pilgrimes*, 1625. See p. 115.

By the second half of the sixteenth century even in France the learned were growing hostile.[1] Though the Trojans were still both fashionable and at times almost orthodox in the seventeenth century, their real influence on historians was over by about 1600.

It would be wrong to dismiss this episode as a mere aberration of the learned and the semi-learned. It was more positive in its results than that. Quite aside from the establishment of a more sure view of ancient history which it provoked in the end, it was in its odd fashion a contribution to the unity of European society. It was possible to argue from the admittedly false premises of the spurious texts that the Turks were in fact not Trojan and that the duty of the Trojans was to combat the Turks.[2] In other words, the peoples of Europe were one, not only in religion, but also by virtue of their descent from a common origin. This, indeed, is the explicit meaning behind Lemaire de Belges's book. His aim, he tells us, was none other than to demonstrate the common origin of the 'two Frances'—Germany and France. 'May God will', he goes on, 'that the armed force of these two noble and powerful nations should be joined amicably together in our time, to recover their heritage Troy, which the Turks occupy.'[3] His final aim is the political welfare of what he more than once calls significantly enough 'nostre Europe',[4] under the leadership of the 'tres hauts Princes de Chrestienté ... affins et alliez ensemble de toute ancienne origine, de la noblesse de Troye'.[5]

Europe and Christendom, as we have noted already, had merged: sixteenth-century indications that this was appreciated are clear and authoritative. In Abraham Ortelius's *Thesaurus geographicus* (1578) we have a telling entry under the word 'Christiani': 'vide Europaei'; and

[1] Joly, pp. 606ff.

[2] Cf. Joly, and T. Spencer, *Fair Greece, Sad Relic*, 1954, pp. 8–12.

[3] *Ed. cit.* ii. 473: 'Or vueille Dieu, que de nostre temps les armes de ces deux tresnobles et trespuissantes nations se puissent ioindre pacifiquement ensemble, pour recouvrer leur heritage de Troye, lequel possedent les Turcz.'

[4] *Ibid.*, i. 350, ii. 260, 463.　　　　　　　　　　　　　　[5] ii. 257.

under 'Europa' we read: 'hodie Christianorum regnum
... Europaei Christianos vocant semet ipsos'.[1] Leonardo
da Vinci, More, Erasmus all make the same assumption.[2]
Early in the seventeenth century Samuel Purchas summed
the matter up:

> Europe is taught the way to scale Heaven, not by Mathematicall
> principles, but by Divine veritie. Jesus Christ is their way, their truth,
> their life; who hath long since given a Bill of Divorce to ingratefull
> Asia where hee was borne, and Africa the place of his flight and
> refuge, and is become almost wholly and onely Europaean. For little
> doe wee find of this name in Asia, lesse in Africa, and nothing at all in
> America, but later Europaean gleanings.[3]

And it was further supported by another survival (like
Noah and Troy) from the past—the Crusade. Clear as it
is that the reiterated statements of sixteenth-century politicians are often window-dressing, it is still the case that
there was a genuine desire for peace in Christian territory
in order to resist the advancing Turk.[4] The papacy might
temporize with the Ottoman Turk, Francis I might seek
the sultan as an ally, but the universal cry of despair at the
loss of Rhodes in 1522 and the general rejoicing over the
victory of Don John of Austria at Lepanto in 1571 indicate a profound consciousness of the unity and function

[1] I quote the revision of 1587: the title of the original is *Synonymia geo-
graphica*.

[2] Leonardo, *Selections from the Notebooks*, ed. I. A. Richter, 1952, p. 248:
'In all parts of Europe there shall be lamentations by great nations for the death
of one man who died in the East [i.e. Jesus].' More, *Utopia*, ed. Lupton,
Oxford 1895, p. 238: 'Etenim in Europa, idque his potissimis partibus quas
CHRISTI fides et religio possidet....' Erasmus, 'In Europae a monachis
subactae picturam', in *Opuscula*, ed. W. K. Ferguson, The Hague 1933, p. 34,
and see C. R. Thompson, 'Erasmus as internationalist and cosmopolitan',
Archiv. für Reformationsgeschichte, xlvi (1955), 167-95 and especially references
to the *Querela Pacis*. A curious example from Italy about 1525 is provided by
the verse of Teofilo Folengo, in his *Il Caos del Triperuno* (*Opere Italiane*, ed.
Renda, i. 307):

> Europa mia, quando fia mai che l'una
> parte di te, c'ha il turco traditore
> rifráncati lo Papa o Imperatore,
> mentri han le chiavi in man, per lor fortuna?

Professor A. Momigliano, who kindly drew my attention to this, points out
the echo of Petrarch's 'Italia mia'.

[3] *Purchas His Pilgrimes*, (Hakluyt Soc., Extra Series), i (1905), p. 251.

[4] G. Mattingly, *Renaissance Diplomacy*, 1955, pp. 164-70.

of Christendom, and transcend a competing tendency for Protestants and Catholics each to link their rival with the Turkish enemy.[1]

The persistence of Christendom—even in face of the all but nugatory crusading impulse—is the most remarkable testimony to its profound hold on the public imagination of the peoples of what was emerging as Europe. 'La chose publique de la chrestienté',[2] the *respublica christiana* of the publicists and the politicians was anything but moribund in the sixteenth century. When defined in purely papalist terms it had few supporters, though it was to preserve the integrity of the 'whole corpes of Christendom' that Thomas More went to the scaffold in 1535.[3] But in a more general and vaguer sense the old concept found adherents and claimed a wide allegiance.

England was in this respect a test case. There the Reformation occurred in an avowedly political context; in an age when princes largely determined public action, it was the English king who broke with Rome; that this pleased many groups of his subjects facilitated his task but did not inspire it. Yet the political reformation in England, which made the sovereign (as More saw clearly it would) a kind of pope, was followed by profound doctrinal innovation from which were to emerge the Church of England and a large body of radical dissenters, who from time to time were very influential. In the second half of the sixteenth century, England, it might seem, had more than many other countries good reason for abandoning Christendom as an outmoded idea. For Catholic Europe, much of it directly threatened by the Turk, the case might be different. And in Protestant Germany the idea of empire might be held to carry with it some emotional association with Christian and oecumeni

[1] Atkinson, *Nouveaux horizons,* p. 234.
[2] Le Maire de Belges, *op. cit.,* ii. 314–5.
[3] Thomas More, *Correspondence,* ed. Elizabeth F. Rogers, Princeton 1947, p. 558.

cal ideas. But in England, attacked at times in strength by the moral and physical forces of the counter Reformation, perched on the Atlantic and looking towards a wider world, the new order might well have been expressed by a rapid assimilation of the new terminology.

That such was not the case we have plentiful evidence, much of it carefully collected and considered by Mr. Le Van Baumer.[1] In general the clergy, as well as princes and diplomats, were faithful to the older tradition. The divines of the Church of England refused to accept responsibility for the destruction of Christian unity; that (if it had been brought about) was the work rather of the Pope. For Hooker in particular England was a part of the Catholic Church, 'a decentralized Christendom ... whose unity was effected by the voluntary consent of the member Churches'.[2] This was formally to be conceived through, on the one hand, a common law of Christendom and, on the other, a general council. The general council was also the device by which Luther and Calvin and other continental reformers protected the ancient fabric of Christian unity: it was 'the ecumenical alternative to the papal monarchy'.[3] In their actual attempts to secure this the divines were, of course, in practice restricted by both the intentions of princely diplomacy and by the divisions which the reformation had forced on both princes and clergy. Rome might be a 'true' church, but as an enemy could not be a 'sound' church. Unity in effect had to be the unity of Protestant churches, or of some of them. These limitations are, of course, fundamental. The Reformation in fact had contributed to the destruction of

[1] In what follows I have derived much help from three essays by F. le Van Baumer, 'The Church of England and the common corps of Christendom', *Journ. of Mod. Hist.*, xvi (1944), 1–21; 'England, the Turk and the common corps of Christendom', *American Hist. Rev.*, l (1944–5), 26–48; 'The conception of Christendom in Renaissance England', *Journ. of the Hist. of Ideas*, vi (1945), 131–56.

[2] Le Van Baumer, 'The Church of England', p. 7.

[3] *Ibid.*, p. 9; and see also Fritzemeyer, pp. 45–70, on the 'renewal of the idea of Christendom in protestantism'.

Christendom. Yet it is important to remember that the English Protestants, in the very moment of disintegration, maintained as their ideal 'the visible Catholic church, and at times they worked hard to realize it'.[1]

In particular the English hierarchy from time to time ordered prayers for (Catholic) Christians threatened by the Turk. Even an anti-Papalist like Fuller was even more an anti-Turk, realizing, not without gratitude, that the safety of the Protestants largely depended on the vigilance of some of the Catholic powers.[2] Purchas, whose identification of Christendom and Europe has just been quoted, whose hostility to the Church of Rome was pronounced, and whose 'hymn to Europe' will be mentioned shortly,[3] thought in the last resort in terms of Christendom. In his will he wrote the following passionate invocation:

Jesus, come quicklie, with the spiritt of grace and power unto thy whole Church; enlarge the bounds thereof to the worlds end and now make it truly Catholike in sinceritie of truth and in extension of thy charitie unto Jewes, Turks, Infidells that thou mayest be the light to enlighten the Gentiles, and the glory of thine Israell; Protect thy people in peace, unite the disagreeinge harts and disioynted states of Christendome, recover those which have fallen by Mahametan impiety and thy servantes which groane under Turkish tyranny. . . . Putt into the harts of Christian princes to hate the whore and love thy spouse, that they may be nursinge Fathers and nursinge mothers to the Israell of God.[4]

As already mentioned, Luther and Calvin were far from denying Christendom, and among continental protestants this was also occasionally reflected in action: the Protestants of Berne, for example, in 1543 prohibited dancing and other frivolities as a mark of compassion for their 'frères Chrétiens' tortured and attacked by the Turks.[5]

As for the diplomats and men of affairs, for them the intrusion of the Turk was a fact which could not be

[1] *Ibid.*, p. 21.
[2] Le Van Baumer, 'England, the Turk, etc.', p. 32.
[3] Below, p. 121.
[4] *Purchas His Pilgrimes*, i, intro., p. 30.
[5] Atkinson, *Nouveaux horizons*, p. 307.

ignored and the practical acceptance of a Moslem state into the field of diplomacy might well have produced an early rejection of Christendom in the field of international relations. Here again we meet a refusal to draw the logical inferences from the situation. The language of diplomacy maintained the established terminology: 'the common enemy, the Christian republic, the Christian world, the provinces of Christendom' are found in the phraseology of a large number of sixteenth- and early seventeenth-century treaties.[1] A similar attitude is found in the treatises of the international lawyers down to, and even beyond, Grotius. If the Turk was not different under natural law, he was certainly different under divine law: the Turk was not far short of a 'natural enemy' of Christians.[2] The diplomats had often to sustain a sorry part. Their princely masters frequently sought the assistance of this 'natural enemy', but were quick to deny the consequences of their actions. Elizabeth of England, for example, did not scruple to try to secure Turkish help against Spain in the 1580s, but in the 1590s was profuse in her explanations that she never had 'the least intent to aid the Turk against Christendom, either directly or indirectly, being a professed Christian Prince'.[3] The project for a Christian league against the Turk was still alive in early Stuart times: the Spanish marriage was justified as promoting 'a holy war against the Turk'; Bacon lent his support to this aim.[4]

Such preoccupations were by no means restricted to Britain. French writers, for example, speak throughout the sixteenth century as frequently, if not more frequently, of 'Chrétiens' and 'Chrétienté', even in contrasts with other parts of the world, than they speak of 'Europe'.[5] The body of Christian states formed the basis of much

---

[1] Le Van Baumer, 'England, the Turk, etc.', 29 e.g. Treaty of Edinburgh, 1560, 'orbisque Christiani quietem'; Treaty of Vervins, 1598, 'Provinces de la Chrestienté'.
[2] Ibid., p. 30.   [3] Ibid., p. 36.   [4] Ibid., p. 46.
[5] Atkinson, Nouveaux horizons, passim.

continental diplomatic activity.[1] Villeroy, in 1608, informed the French ambassador in London, that the situation was propitious for the establishment of 'une paix universelle en la chrétienté'[2] and Sully's 'grand dessein' as it gradually took shape was based directly on religious assumptions common to the Catholic, Lutheran and Calvinist communities he accepted as a permanent feature of his world. Turkey was excluded from the universal peace Sully envisaged for 'les peuples tres-chrestiens de l'Europe' and the general council of member states would have disposed of a huge armada destined to attack the enemy of Christendom.[3]

The vitality of Christendom thus extended well into the seventeenth century. Identified as it had been with Europe, Christendom was virtually interchangeable with Europe for all the sixteenth century and for much of the seventeenth. For Pascal (to take an example at random) there seems to be no difference between the two concepts.[4] This limitation of Christian communities to a European homeland was clearly revealed in what seems to be the first map of world religions. This was engraved by Josse Hondius and appeared in the 1625 edition of *Purchas His Pilgrimes* (plate V). Ingenious in its construction, this is the map of the Christian world we have sought for in vain during the Middle Ages[5]. It cannot be said to present a comforting picture of the spread of the Christian faith.[6] So far as territory was concerned Christians were in succeeding centuries to be masters of areas much greater

---

[1] Armando Saitta, *Dalla Res Publica Christiana agli Stati Uniti di Europa,* Rome 1948, pp. 23–59.   [2] *Ibid.,* p. 25.   [3] *Ibid.,* pp. 42–57.

[4] *Pensées,* I. v. 8; vi. 7. The same is true earlier of Bodin: 'potentats chrétiens' means the same as 'princes d'Europe' in the *République.*

[5] See above, p. 55.

[6] The scale of reproduction possible in this book makes it hard to see the symbols used by Hondius. They are: † = Christianity, Ⴗ = Mahometanism ↑ = idolatry. The Christian and Islamic symbols are thus clearly derived from earlier cartographical practice (above p. 93f.); perhaps the arrow of the idolaters derives from the use of this in those continental figures mentioned already as in use for geographical description (p. 104).

than the old Christendom of the past. Their conquests were, however, hardly regarded as those of a religion. In the course of the seventeenth and early eighteenth centuries Christendom slowly entered the limbo of archaic words and Europe emerged as the unchallenged symbol of the largest human loyalty.

CHAPTER 7

THE PROSPECT OF EUROPE

WHEN Lemaire de Belges is found referring in a proprietorial way to 'nostre Europe'—and he was not the only writer to use the phrase, even in the early sixteenth century[1]—it is clear that the notion has acquired a positive meaning which it hardly possessed in the middle ages. In the course of the seventeenth century the processes which had led to this result were finally brought to a conclusion.[2] By the beginning of the eighteenth century it is in terms of Europe that Europeans view the world. This may be neatly illustrated by the terminology of two documents of parallel origin and intention. In giving Cabot his patent in 1496 the king of England commissioned him to explore for lands hitherto 'unknown to all Christians'[3]; in 1764 Commodore John Byron was ordered to look for 'lands and islands of great extent hitherto unvisited by any European power'.[4] The final stages in this development may be traced in a wealth of material which cannot be surveyed here. Much of it has, however, been discussed by others[5] and the remaining

---

[1] E.g., Gemma Phrysius (1530) in Apian's *Cosmographia* (1533) says of Florida and other newly found territories that they are 'nostra Europa non multo inferior'; quoted Taylor, *Tudor Geography*, p. 274.

[2] See Paul Hazard, *La crise de la conscience europienne*, 2 vols., Paris 1935, esp. i. 3-37, 70-104.

[3] J. A. Williamson, *Voyages of the Cabots* (1929), quoted by J. N. L. Baker, *A History of Geographical Discovery and Exploration*, 1937, p. 83.

[4] *Ibid.*, p. 159.

[5] Fritzemeyer, pp. 91-165, deals especially with French political speculation, Grotius, Hobbes, Spinoza and Leibniz; F. Chabod, 'L'idea di Europa', *La Rassegna d'Italia*, ii (1947), 3-17, 25-37 is a much wider survey, coming down to the nineteenth century: there is also useful material and reflection in A. Saitta's book, above, p. 115 n. 1. The most elaborate treatment of the later material is by Heinz Gollwitzer, *Europabild und Europagedanke*, Munich 1951, in which there is a very full study particularly of German writers in the

pages of this essay will be devoted mainly to a summary of their conclusions, together with a brief discussion of the boundaries of Europe as they were viewed in the Renaissance period.

Europe was politically drawn together by the house of Hapsburg before 1648 and after 1648 by the house of Bourbon. In both cases the existence of an aggressive and powerful dynasty seemed to contemporaries to demand concerted efforts if the liberty and independence of other states were to be secured. There is accordingly a practical unity about the European political scene in the seventeenth century which it had lacked earlier, at any rate before the second half of the sixteenth century. The Franco-English hostilities of the later middle ages, the state 'system' of *quattrocento* Italy, the affairs of Germany under Frederick III and Maximilian, are disparate *foci* of interest, only transiently linked one to another. Even the hostility of Francis I and Charles V, though it came near to absorbing other major rivalries, hardly did so in the lifetime of the two combatants: the notion of a 'balance of power' in the first half of the sixteenth century was not one actively adopted by contemporaries.[1] But the consequences of Charles V's empire was in the long run a general fear of the Hapsburgs, to be followed by the growth of a general fear of France. Practical politics and political idealism both reflected these preoccupations and thereby contributed to the further self-awareness of Europe. Lingering loyalty to the older scheme of things prevents this from being at once reflected in the language of diplomacy and the last treaty to include a reference to the 'Respublica Christiana' was Utrecht, in 1714.[2]

Even on the plane of the narrowest self-interest, politicians in the seventeenth century could conjure with the idea of Europe. A good example of this is the play by

eighteenth and nineteenth centuries. Paolo Brezzi, *Realtà e Mito dell' Europa* (Rome 1955), is a slighter survey and also deals mainly with the later period.

[1] Mattingly, *Renaissance Diplomacy*, pp. 162-80.

[2] Mattingly, *op. cit.*, p. 301 note 1.

Demarets de Saint-Sorlin which was written about 1642 and which overtly displayed Richelieu's policy. *Europe* was not a successful play, but it is none the less symptomatic that a statesman should interest himself in propagating his hostility to Spain (the 'Ibère' of the play) in terms which some generations earlier would have seemed purely mythological. 'Europe', the princess, is full of concern for all her children (and it is stressed that all the nations are of common stock) but chooses to be defended by 'Francion'. It was a programme of a European peace in which peace would be kept by an alert and powerful, but beneficent and disinterested, France.[1]

The writers for whom universal peace was a genuine programme also encouraged the further evolution of the consciousness of Europe. A curious aspect of an idealized European unity may be seen in the distorted 'map' of Europe in the form of a queen which was published in late sixteenth- and early seventeenth-century reprints of Münster's *Cosmographia* (see Frontispiece).[2] Such iconographical ingenuity merely reflected more sober speculation. At the start of the seventeenth century, as we have seen, Sully's project of peace covered the 'peuples tres-Chrestiens de l'Europe'; and at the other end of it we have William Penn's *Essay towards the Present and Future Peace of Europe* (1693).[3] The chief monument of this attempt by idealists to 'institutionalize' the notion of Europe came, of course, in the early decades of the next century with the Abbé de Saint-Pierre, whose first work on the subject, *Mémoires pour rendre la paix perpetuelle en Europe*, appeared in 1712.[4]

[1] E. J. Najam, '*Europe*: Richelieu's blueprint for unity and peace', *Studies in Philology*, liii (1956), 25-34; cf. Fritzemeyer, p. 100ff.

[2] The Basle edition of 1588 was apparently the first (fo. xli). See above, pp. 105-6, and R. Salomon, *Opicinus*, i. 66-7 and notes, where some examples of seventeenth-century depictions of countries are quoted. Mr. Donald Nicoll drew my attention to the reproduction of this figure in *The Tablet* for 5 March 1955, where it is accompanied by a rather misleading description, based on the assumption that it appeared in Münster's lifetime.

[3] Saitta, p. 59.   [4] *Ibid.*, pp. 63-83.

The acceptance of the European peoples as politically one would nevertheless have been (we may assume) of limited significance if at the same time there had not developed a sense of cultural unity. Unquestionably the most important single element in the creation of this sentiment was that identification of Christendom and Europe which we have already noted, and which was further enriched by seventeenth-century thinkers such as Leibniz.[1] When Purchas wrote of Jesus Christ as 'almost wholly and onely Europaean'[2] he was summarizing not merely a historical process, but the awareness of it. We have moved from the fact to the consciousness of the fact.[3]

Purchas, however, goes far further in his analysis. He repeats and elaborates the advantages of the geography and climate of the continent: 'The Qualitie of Europe exceeds her Quantitie, in this the least, in that the best of the World.'[4] This notion, which as we have seen goes back to ancient times, has an intensity and an actuality by the end of the sixteenth century which makes it far more than a merely literary commonplace. Besides the advantages which nature, through divine providence and the industry of man, has given the region, 'as it were conspiring the European good', it has other attributes. Where else do we find, he writes, such 'resolute courages, able bodies, well qualified mindes'? What other area is so 'fortified with Castles, edified with Townes, crowned with Cities'. And has not the whole universe fallen before the European mastery?—Asia and Africa were 'captivated', the first by Alexander and both by the Romans. As for America she has been made 'tributary and servant' by 'Spanish and Portugall Discoveries and Conquests':

All and more then they all, since and still made open and obnoxious to the English and Dutch, which have discovered new Northerne Worlds, and in their thrice-worthy Marine Armes have so often imbraced the inferiour Globe. Asia yeerely sends us her Spices, Silkes

[1] Fritzemeyer, pp. 152–65.   [2] Above, p. 110.
[3] Chabod, *loc. cit.*   [4] *Purchas his Pilgrimes*, p. 248.

and Gemmes; Africa her Gold and Ivory; America receiveth severer Customers and Tax-Masters, almost everywhere admitting Europaean Colonies.[1]

Thus in practice Europe dominates the world. But this is not all.

Europe is the sole home of the 'Arts and Inventions' which 'are mens properest goods, immortal Inheritance to our mortalitie', that is, which distinguish man from brute creation. 'The Liberall Arts are most liberall to us, having long since forsaken their Seminaries in Asia and Afrike': for one Athens overthrown by the Turks, 'how many many Christian Athenses have wee in the West for it'. As for 'Mechanical Sciences' Europe has given birth to 'the many artificiall Mazes and Labyrinths in our Watches'. 'What eares but Europaean have heard so many Musicall Inventions for the Chamber, the Field, the Church?' In the arts of cooking, horse management, chemistry, Europe is pre-eminent. Paper and mills for all purposes, guns, printing are all European, and so are perpetual motion, squaring the circle and 'innumerable other Mathematicall and Chymicall devises'. 'Alas, China yeelds babes and bables in both [printing and gunpowder] compared with us and ours: the rest of the World have them borrowed of us or not at all.'[2]

For Purchas there was a further evidence of European majesty—exploration:

But what speke I of Men, Arts, Armes? Nature hath yeelded her selfe to Europaean Industry. Who ever found out that Loadstone and Compasse, that findes out and compasseth the World? Who ever tooke possession of the Ocean, and made procession round about the vast Earth? Who ever discovered new Constellations, saluted the Frozen Poles, subjected the Burning Zones? And who else by the Art of Navigation have seemed to imitate Him, which laies the beames of his Chambers in the Waters, and walketh on the wings of the Wind?[3]

And the author then proceeds to his enunciation of Christ's European mission.[4] The rhetoric of Purchas is infectious

---

[1] *Purchas his Pilgrimes*, p. 249. [2] *Ibid.*, pp. 249-50.
[3] *Ibid.*, pp. 250-1. [4] Above.

and unguarded. Perhaps the most telling thing about the passages just quoted is their use of 'us, ours' to mean, simply, European. With this we must compare that early usage of 'nostri' to mean Christian,[1] characteristic of an attitude of mind now patently archaic.

At a more sophisticated level also the period advanced towards similar conclusions. Political thought after the thirteenth century found increasing use for Aristotle's division between the rule of law in Africa and the despotism of Asia, though an aversion for the non-classical word 'despotus' on the part of the humanists led by Bruni sometimes blurred the distinction.[2] A fresh start along the same line of reasoning is probably to be found in Machiavelli, where the notion of Europe as a community with specifically secular as opposed to religious characteristics is given clear expression.[3] There are more good soldiers in Africa or Asia because in Europe there are many republics and several kingdoms, whereas in Africa or Asia there are only one or two kingdoms and few republics. There is more *virtù* where there are more states which favour it. The Turkish form of government is to have one chief and the rest slaves; in the West the barons owe their position not to the whims of a prince but to inheritance. So Europe and Asia present two different types of political organization, and 'this is a difference rich in consequences, for the multiplicity of states encourages the development of *virtù*, that is the capacity for action, the creative energy of the individual'.[4]

These notions are the direct antecedents of the completely developed 'Europeanism' of Montesquieu, for whom, in brief, Europe represented progress, Asia stagnation.[5] Europe, composed of many states, ideally 'balanced', is the home of liberty. Europe, in the words of Voltaire, for long has been:

[1] Above, pp. 56-7.
[2] Koebner (cit. above, p. 38 n. 3), pp. 282-5.
[3] *Arte della guerra*, ii, and *Principe*, iv. See Chabod p. 7 and cf. above, p. 105.
[4] Chabod, *loc. cit.*   [5] *Ibid.*, p. 12.

a kind of great republic divided into several states, some monarchical, the others mixed; the former aristocratic, the latter popular; but all corresponding with one another. They all have the same religious foundation, even if divided into several confessions. They all have the same principle of public law and politics, unknown in the other parts of the world.[1]

Divorced now by eighteenth-century illuminism from its association with Christendom, and fortified by the notion of a 'republic of letters', itself the product of medieval education, by the *diaspora* of Italian humanists and the later dispersion of the Huguenots, the sentiment of European unity was thus married to the interlocking political affairs of the continent referred to at the start of this chapter. 'No European', said Burke in 1796, 'can be a complete exile in any part of Europe.'[2]

With these words of Burke we come to the final realization of the idea of Europe. There yet remains a not unimportant aspect of the question: what exactly were the boundaries of the area which, in the late Renaissance, thus took stock of itself?

The eastern limits of the continent had been fixed for a thousand years at the frontier of the Don. On the whole Renaissance geographers were content with this. Fra Mauro in 1459 drew attention to the opinion that the Volga was a truer division between Europe and Asia[3]; Ortelius a century later advanced the river Ob as a boundary.[4] But the atlases, rapidly multiplying in the late sixteenth and seventeenth centuries, adhered to the traditional line of demarcation.

Of more interest are the doubts expressed about the main consequence of the old division: its inclusion of Russia in Europe. This had small importance so long as

---

[1] *Siècle de Louis XIV*, quoted Saitta, p. 101.

[2] *Letters on the Regicide Peace*, quoted Chabod, p. 3.

[3] Mansuy, *Le Monde Slave*, p. 10.

[4] A. Ortelius, *Theatrum orbis terrarum*, Antwerp 1573, map 61 (Europe); though the text in this edition adheres to the Don this boundary is enlarged northward to the Ob in the text in the (posthumous) edition of 1624, at fo. x.

Europe was a mere name on a map. It began to have direct relevance with the emergence of Europe as a symbol of a way of life, which in any case coincided with a considerable increase in western knowledge about Russia. For Rabelais, it seems, there is conflict: the Russians are eastwards-looking; even if they are European by origin they are Asiatic by inclination; it is even doubtful if Moscow is in Europe or in Asia. And in Hondius's map (above p. 115 and plate V) the region needed the symbols of Christianity, Islam and idolatry. Such doubts were only partly resolved as the Tartar menace declined and as the Slav Russians embarked on a closer association with the European west.[1] Even if it was accepted that Russia was populated in the first place by 'Scythians' stemming from the progeny of Japheth it nonetheless seemed, even in the seventeenth century, essentially an oriental country[2]; Sully excluded Russia, as he excluded the Turks, from his *grand dessein*; the Russians occupied more of Asia than they did of Europe, they were wilder and in general different in character from Europeans; many of them were still heathen, they were far away from Europe, and even among Christian Russians a different Christian tradition was a barrier to mutual understanding.[3]

The rapidity with which Russia was assimilated increased at the end of the seventeenth century with Peter the Great, for he not only intensified the participation of Russia in European politics, he made it his aim to 'civilize' his country on the pattern of the West. Penn accepted the Russians into his pacifist programme—but then he also accepted the Turks. The Abbé de Saint-Pierre, on the other hand, rejected the Turks, but accepted the Russians.[4] For Voltaire Peter the Great had civilized his country and Montesquieu said of him that he had 'given

---

[1] Mansuy, pp. 13-16. Cf. F. Braudel, *La Méditerranée et le monde méditerranéen a l'époque de Philippe II*, Paris 1949, pp. 146-7.

[2] M. S. Anderson, 'English views of Russia in the XVII century', *Slavonic and East European Review*, xxxiii (1954), 140-60, and esp. pp. 147, 157 and refs.

[3] Saitta, pp. 53-4.   [4] *Ibid.*, pp. 59, 72.

the manners of Europe to a European nation'.[1] There remained difficulties. If, by the start of the eighteenth century, Europe was coming to stand for 'freedom' as against oriental 'despotism', it was hard not to range Russia among 'despotic' powers. Montesquieu was aware of the difficulty.[2] Frederick the Great remained sceptical about Russia's right to a place among civilized powers.[3]

The final stage came with the Napoleonic wars and the peace settlement thereafter. Russia's part in this was too big to be ignored. And during the conference period the geographers took cognisance of the new world. In 1833 Volger, in his *Handbuch der Geographie*, produced the boundary at the river Ural and the Ural mountains which was to remain the nineteenth-century boundary of 'Russia in Europe, Russia in Asia'.[4] A final shape had been given to the Europe whose spiritual content had been gradually defined in the centuries between Petrarch and Montesquieu.

Christendom, which was potentially the world, had been replaced by Europe. Europe, inheritor of Christianity, heir of a religion oecumenical in its aims, seems in comparison a concept circumscribed in place and time, a region rather than a programme. Yet paradoxically in and after the eighteenth century Europe was to achieve a universal, if temporary, dominance in the world which had been denied to Christendom. The name of a continent was then to grow into a symbol of a way of life and was to prove, no less than the faith which had preceded it, capable of attracting loyalties and hatreds, missionaries and martyrs.

[1] *Esprit des lois*, xix, ch. 4, quoted Chabod p. 28 n. 94, q.v. for the refs. to Voltaire and a useful general discussion. Russia was listed among European powers for the first time in 1716 in the *Almanach royal*.

[2] *Esprit des lois*, xii, ch. 18; xiii, ch. 6; in Chabod, *loc. cit.*

[3] *Oeuvres*, Berlin 1846, ii. 23-4, 49, in Chabod, *loc. cit.*

[4] F. G. Hahn, 'Zur Geschichte der Grenze zwischen Europa und Asien', *Mitteilungen des Vereins für Erdkunde zu Leipzig* (1881), 83-104 and maps. Earlier attempts to find a suitable boundary are discussed and illustrated in this paper.

INDEX

Adam of Bremen, 35 n. 7, 52 n. 6
Aemilius, Paulus, 101
Aethelwerd, 47
Africa, 2, 4, 9 n. 3, 10, 12, 14-15, 32, 122; Christians in, 20, 66; personified, 104; *and see* Ham
Aimoin, 49 n. 1
Albertus Magnus, 38
Alcuin, 38-9
Alexander, 4, 5
Alexandria, 66
Alexis IV, emperor, 35
Alfred, king, 47-8
America, 99; personified, 104
Andrew, St., apostle, 40
Andrews, M. C., collection of *mappaemundi*, 53 n. 6
Angelôme of Luxeuil, 39
Anglo-Saxon Chronicle, 47
Annius of Viterbo, 108
Anselm of Laon, 40
Apianus, P., 100, 105
Apostles, dispersion of, 34, 40, 42, 54
Arbela, battle of, 5
Arian Christianity, 17-19
Aristotle, 3, 5-6, 38, 122
Arthur, king, *see* English
Asia, 2, 5, 10, 12, 14, 32, 39, 122; Christians in, 20, 65-6, 85; personified, 5, 104; *and see* Shem
'Asiatic', 3-4
Asser, 47
Augustine, St., 10-12, 13-14, 21, 23, 28, 33, 39, 42
Avignon popes, 62, 68, 73-6

Babel, Tower of, 10 n. 1, 108

Bacon, Sir Francis, 114
Bacon, Roger, 24, 82n., 94
Balbi, G., 86
Barbarians, 4, 16-19; Barbarism, concept of 23-4, 33
Bartholomew, St., apostle, 40
Basin, T., 88-9
Basle, council of, 82
Bayezid I, sultan, 68
Bayezid II, sultan, 89
'Beatus' maps, 54
Beauvais, Vincent of, 38
Bede, 28, 37, 38
Bellini, G., 103 n. 2
Benedict XII, pope, 78
Benedict XIII, pope, 69
Berne, 113
Bible and cosmography, 7-8; *see* Genesis
Black Sea, 2
Boccaccio, 14 n. 5, 86-7
Bodin, J., 115 n. 4
Boissard, J.-J., 100
Bonet, Honoré, 76 n. 3
Boniface, VIII, pope, 61
Bonnivard, 107
Bourbon, family, 118
Bourgueil, Baudri de, 50
British, legendary origins of, 43-9
Brutus, *see* English
Burke, E., 123
Byron, John, 117
Byzantine Empire, 16-17, 30
Byzantium, *see* Greek Empire

Cabot, 117
Calvin, 112-13
Camoens, 105
Canistris, Opicinus de, 55 n. 2
'Carthaginian', 4 n. 1

Cartography:
  Greek and Roman, 5-7; *peri-
    ploi*, 6; *Mappaemundi*, 53-5,
    94-5; *Portolani*, 90ff; and
    Dante, 92; Europe identified
    with Christendom, 94; Chris-
    endom and, 115-16
Celtic Christianity, 18-19
Celtis, Conrad, 101
Cervantes, 102
Chadwick, H. M., 47
Chansons de Geste, 57
Charlemagne, 21, 51-2, 102
Charles V, emperor, 104, 118
Charles VI, king of France, 69
Charles VII, king of France, 82
Charles Martel, 25
Chastellain, G., 88
Christendom, Christianitas: in
    Latin and vernaculars, 22-3,
    27-36, 87-8; ambiguities con-
    cerning, 22-3; and non-
    Christian world, 23; concept
    strengthened by attack, 24ff;
    political obligations, 26
  in Early Middle Ages, 27-36,
    41, 55; universal mission, 27;
    notion of, 28, 29; Seljuk
    threat and Council of Cler-
    mont, 30; Pope as head of, 35;
    in late Middle Ages, 56-83;
    European contrasted with
    overseas, 57-60; 14th century
    fragmentation of, 66; alter-
    ation in boundaries, 77;
    respublica Christiana, 87
  in Renaissance, 96-7, 111-16,
    120; identified with Europe,
    115-116; in maps, 94-5; in
    literature, 109-10; persistence
    of concepts, 111ff
'Christian', 56; *see* 'Nostri'
Church, Christian:
  Arian and Latin, 17-19; Latin
    and Greek, 19-20, 51-2; dis-
    tinct from world, 21; terri-
    torial nature, 30; oecumenical
    character, 34-6, 40; transcen-
    dental, 11, 42; and Dante,

Church, Christian (*contd.*)
    59-60; in 14th century, 61ff;
    Asian, 65-6; Nestorian, 65;
    Coptic, 66; Papal schsim, 68ff;
    international orders in, 70;
    decentralization, 96ff; Luth-
    eran crisis, 97
Civil law, 63-4
Clari, Robert de, 57 n. 1
Clement VII, pope, 69
Clermont, Council of, 30-3
Climate, influence of, 5, 32-3, 38,
    120
Clovis, 18
Colonna, Francesco, 103
Columban, St., 28
Comestor, Petrus, 43
Commerce, unifying effects of,
    67-8
Commynes, P., 89
Comnena, Anna, 51 n. 1
Conches, William of, 54
Constance, Council of, 69, 71,
    77-82, 97
Constantinople, 17, 35, 82-3; *and
    see* Byzantine Empire
Continents, in Renaissance litera-
    ture, 101-2; in Renaissance
    art, 104; maps of, *see* Carto-
    graphy; *see* Africa, America,
    Asia, Europe, Libya
Coptic church, *see* Africa, Chris-
    tians in
Corvinus, Matthias, 89
Cosmas Indicopleustes, 13
Cosmopolitanism, 33
Crete and mythical Europa, 1
Crusade, idea of, 26, 29-34, 50,
    56-7, 81-2, 85, 110-11
Cursor Mundi, 41, 60

Dante, 59-60, 64 n. 2, 86, 92-3
Dati, Leonardo, 92
'Divisio apostolorum', *see* Apostles
Don (Tanais) river, 2, 7, 123
Donne, J., 102 n. 4
Dubois, Pierre, 36 n.
Dudo of Saint Quentin, 49
Dürer, 103

East, knowledge of the, in the XVI century, 99

East-West polarity, 2-3, 50-1

Ebsdorf, wall map at, 94

Eden, garden of, 8

Edward I, king of England, 61

Edward III, king of England, 62, 98

Eliot, John, 107

Elizabeth, queen, 114

Empire, Roman:
  Extension, 4; supracontinental nature, 16; decentralization, 16; Germanic invasions, 17; religious unification, 20; survival and values, 21; 'Roman' and 'Christian', 23, 34-5; and Charlemagne, 51-2; and Gregory VII, 52; in XIII and XIV centuries, 63-4; a part of Europe, 79

England, church in, 69-72, 97-8; at council of Constance, 77-80; church of, 112-13; and Renaissance Christendom, 111-14

English, mythical origins of, 43-8

Erasmus, 101, 106, 110

Eratosthenes, 6

Estienne, R., 101

Eucher, St., 13

Eugenius IV, pope, 82

Eulogium historiarum, 42, 49 n. 4

Europa, myth of, 1, 14 n. 5, 42; iconography of, in ancient art, 5; in medieval art, 53; in Renaissance art, 103

Europe: suggested etymologies, 1; territorial meaning, 2; boundaries, 2, 123-5; superiority, 3
  significance to Greeks and Romans, 4; to Jews and early Christians, 9-14; and Japheth's progeny, 10-14; land of Gentiles, Greeks and Christians, 14; Germanic tribes converted, 18; Christian unification, 20; unity

Europe, significance (*contd.*)
  under attack, 25; and Urban II, 32
  significance in Middle Ages, 32, 37-55; legendary founders of races of, 43ff; genealogy of descent from Japheth, 45; Trojan legend and, 48; and Charlemagne, 52; démodé in 11th century, 52; devoid of sentiment, 58; increasing significance in 14th century, 59
  significance in Renaissance, 73-107, 109-10, 117-231; land of Christians, 75, 80; and Pius II, 84-87; growth of term, 100-101, 105-6; and Hapsburgs, 118; cultural unity of, 120; final contrast with Asia, 121-22

Europe, personified: in ancient art, 5 and n.; in Renaissance, 104, 119; *and see* Cartography

'Europe', 'European', in Latin and vernaculars, 25, 56-9, 86-90, 100-2, 106-7

Falkenberg, 81

Fillastre, G., 78 n. 1

Flores historiarum, 42

Folengo, T., 110 n. 2

France, 74-6; church in, 69-72, 98; at Constance, 77-80; and Renaissance Christendom, 114-15; and idea of Europe, 119

Francis I, king of France, 110, 118

Franken, Frans, the younger, 104

Franks, legendary origin of, 48-50, 108-9

Fredegarius, 48-50

Frederick III, emperor, 118

Frederick the Great, 125

Freducci family, 94 n. 1

Fries, Lorenz, 100

Fuller, 113

Gaguin, R., 89-90

Galle, Ph., 104

Gallicanism, *see* France, church in

Genealogy:
European nations, 93ff; British tradition, 43-6; English tradition, 47-8; Trojan origins, 48ff

Genesis story of Noah, 8-14, 38-48, 107-8

Gentiles, 12, 14

Geography, Greek, 2-3; medieval, 37-8, 53-5; late medieval, 90-5; Renaissance, 99-100, 104; *and see* Cartography

Germain, Jean, 82-3

Germany, 63-4; church in 71, 97-8

Gog and Magog, 8

Granada, reconquest of, 64-5, 81

Grandes Chroniques de France, 50, 58, 60

Greek Church, 19-20, 28, 30, 34, 56-7, 82

Greek Empire, 51-3, 84

Gregoras, Nikephorus, 91

Gregory the Great, pope, 19, 23, 28

Gregory VII, pope, 29, 35, 52, 106

Gregory XI, pope, 68

Gregory of Tours, 48

Habitus praecipuorum populorum, 100, 104

Ham, 8-14, 38-48, 103, 107-8

Hapsburg family, 118

Hecataeus of Miletus, 2

Hedwiga, 64

Henri III, king of France, 102

Henry I, emperor, 52

Henry VII, emperor, 64 n. 2

Henry IV, king of England, 22, 69

Henry V, king of England, 69, 78

Henry VIII, king of England, 97-8

Heraldic cartography, 93-5

Hereford, wall map at, 54, 94

Heresy, in later Middle Ages, 63

Herodotus, 2-3, 6, 23

Higden, Ranulf, 38, 42, 49, 58-9

Hincmar, 29

Hippocrates, school of, 3, 5

Hondius, J., 115-16, 124

Hooker, Richard, 112

Humanist style, 87-8

Hundred Years War, 82-3

Huntingdon, Henry of, 49

Hunyadi, John, 82

Hymn to Apollo, 1

Influences of Atmosphere, etc., 3

Innocent III, pope, 35, 106

Ionithus, 42-3

Isaiah, 7

Isidor Pacensis, 25

Isidore of Seville, 13-14, 37, 38, 42, 54

Islam, expansion of, 24-6, 30, 65, 66; *see* Turks

Isocrates, 3, 5

Italy, 63-4

Jacobites, *see* Asia, Christians in

Jagiello, 64

James, St., apostle, 40

James V, king of Scotland, 98

Japheth, in patristic period, 8-14; in medieval period, 38-48, 74-5; in Renaissance, 107-8; iconography, 103

Jerome, St., 9 n. 1, 12-13, 39, 44, 48

Jerusalem, 8, 26, 30, 34-5, 81

Jews, and cosmographical notions, 7-8

John, St., apostle, 27, 40

John VIII, pope, 29

John XXII, pope, 63

Jornandes, 47 n. 2

Josephus, 9-10, 14, 44

Justinian, 16-17

Lactantius, 12

Latin Christianity, *see* Roman church

Latini, Brunetto, 38

Laurana, F., 95 n. 4

Lemaire de Belges, 107-8

Lepanto, battle of, 110

Libya, 2, 4, 13

Lithuania, conversion of, 64-5, 81-2
Lullingstone, Roman villa at, 5 n. 2
Luther, 97, 112-13

Machiavelli, 105, 122
Macrobius, 54
Mahomet, 24
Mahomet, the Conqueror, sultan, 83-4
Major, John, 101
Malmesbury, William of, 31-4, 40, 47 n. 6
Mandeville, Sir John, 38, 66
Mappaemundi, Maps, *see* Cartography
Marot, Clément, 101
Marseilles, 75
Martianus Capella, 37
Martin V, pope, 69
Marullus, 101 n. 8
Matthew, St., apostle, 40
Matthias, St., apostle, 40
Maur, Raban, 40
Mauro, Fra, 123
Maximilian, emperor, 118
Mediterranean sea, 4, 6-7
Mercator, 100
Methodius, St., 42-3
Michow, M. à, 106
Milton, John, 102 n. 5
Mistère du viel Testament, 103 n. 2
Mommsen, 44
Mongols, 65-6
Monmouth, Geoffrey of, 49
Monophysites, *see* Africa, Christians in
Montesquieu, 122, 124-5
Morbeke, William, 38
More, Sir T., 110-11
Morea, despot of the, 85
Münster, Sebastian, 105-6, 119

National churches, 61-3, 69-72, 77, 96-8
Nennius, 43-6
Nestorians, *see* Asia, church in
Nicholas I, pope, 29

Nile river, 2, 4, 7
Noah, the Genesis account, 8-9; in patristic period, 10-14; in middle ages, 38-48; in Renaissance, 107-8; iconography of 5, 3, 103
Nogent, Guibert of, 30 n. 2, 34 n. 2
'Nostre Europe', 117
'Nostri', 5, 6-7, 122
'Nostrum mare', 4; *see* Mediterranean

Ob river, 123
Orders, religious, in later middle ages, 70
Orosius, 10, 13, 37
Ortelius, A., 109-10, 123
Otto III, emperor, 24
Otto of Freising, 34-5, 40, 51
'Outremer', 57, 60
Overseas expansion, its consequences, 99-100
Ovid, 103

Papacy, 29-35, 110-111; and spread of Christianity, 19; and Carolingian theocracy, 52; and nationalism, 61ff; Schism, 68ff; and Council of Constance, 76-7
Paris, Matthew, 40 n. 1, 42, 48, 57-8
Pascal, 115
Pasquier, E., 102
Paul St., apostle, 27, 40
Peace and idea of Europe, 119
Penn, W., 119, 124
Periploi, 6
Persia, opposition to Greece, 3-4
Peter, St., apostle, 40
Peter the Great, 124
Peter the Venerable, 40 n. 3
Petrarch, 59-60, 73-4, 84-5
Peutinger tables, 6
Phasis river, 2
Philip, St., apostle, 40
Philip IV, king of France, 61
Phrysius, G., 100 n. 1, 117 n. 1

Piccolomini, Aeneas Sylvius, *see* Pius II

Pirckheimer, W., 100

Pisa, Council of, 69

Pius II, pope, 83-7, 96, 100, 105

Platina, B., 100

Pliny, 38

Poland, 81-2

Polo, Marco, 38

Portolan charts, 90-95

Proverbs, Book of, 7-8

Prussia, 81

Ptolemy, 6-7, 99-100

Purchas, Samuel, 110, 113, 120-2

Rabelais, 124

Radbert, Paschasius, 40

Raleigh, Sir Walter, 108

Ramusio, 107

Red Sea, 4

Reform of Church, in later middle ages, 70-1, 77

Reformation, 97; and Christendom, 111-15

Rémy of St. Germain d'Auxerre, 39 n. 5

Reunion of the churches, 66, 82

Rhodes, 110

Richard II, king of England, 69

Richelieu, 119

Ripa, 104

Robert of Tuy, 41

Roland, Song of, 26

Roman church, 17, 34-6, 56-7, 96-8, 112-13

Roman Empire, *see* Empire

Rome, sack of by the Saracens, 25; and papacy in XIV cent., 73-5

Ronsard, P., 101-2

Rous, J., 22 n. 2

Rucellai, G., 22 n. 2

Russia, 64-5; and Europe, 123-5

St. Albans, Boke of, 107

St. Albans, chronicles at, 42, 48

Saint-Denis, *see Grandes Chroniques*

Saint-Maure, Benoît de, 49

Saint-Pierre, Abbé de, 119, 124

Saint-Sorlin, Desmarets de, 119

St. Victor, Hugh of, 39

Sallust, 54

Salonika, 82

Sanudo, Marino, 92

Schedel, H., 103 n. 2

Schism, of 1378, its effects, 68-72

Scotland, church in, 98

Servetus, M., 100

Shem, 8-14, 38-8, 103, 107

Sigismund, emperor, 69

Simon, St., apostle, 40

Social status, and the progeny of Noah, 41-2, 107

Solinus, 4 n. 2, 7

Spain, 64-5; church in, 98

Sperando of Mantua, 95 n. 4

Strabo, 3, 6

Suez, 2

Sully, 115, 119, 124

Tacitus, 46

'Teucri', *see* Turks

Teutonic knights, 81

Thaddaeus, St., (Jude), apostle, 40

Thomas, St., apostle, 40

Timurlenk, 68

Titian, 103

Tours, battle of, 25

Trebizond, 85

Trithemius, John, 108

Trojan legend, ancestors of Franks, 48-9; and Brutus, 49; Turks, 48, 50, 84-5; in XVI cent., 108-9

Turks, legendary Trojan origins of, 48, 50, 84-5, 109; Seljuk, 26, 30, 50; Ottoman, 65-8, 82; and Christendom, 110-11, 113-15, 122, 124

Ural river and mountains, 125

Urban II, pope, 29-34, 37, 40

Urban V, pope, 74

Urban VI, pope, 68-9

Utrecht, treaty of, 118

Vadianus, J., 100

Van Baumer, F. le, 112
Vergil, Polydore, 101
Veronese, 103
Vespucci, Amerigo, 105
Villeroy, 115
Vinci, Leonardo da, 110
Virgil, 44
Vladimiri, Paulus, 81
Volga river, 123
Volger, 125
Voltaire, 122-4

Waldseemüller, 99-100
Walsperger, A., 93
Walther von der Vogelweide, 22 n. 3
Wendover, Roger, 42
West, opposed to East see East-West
Widukind of Corvey, 49 n. 1, 52
Wycliffe, J., 97

Young, Richard, 76